How to Think About Catastrophe

STUDIES IN VIOLENCE, MIMESIS, AND CULTURE

SERIES EDITOR
William A. Johnsen

The Studies in Violence, Mimesis, and Culture Series examines issues related to the nexus of violence and religion in the genesis and maintenance of culture. It furthers the agenda of the Colloquium on Violence and Religion, an international association that draws inspiration from René Girard's mimetic hypothesis on the relationship between violence and religion, elaborated in a stunning series of books written over a period of more than forty years. Readers interested in this area of research can also look to the association's journal, *Contagion: Journal of Violence, Mimesis, and Culture.*

ADVISORY BOARD

René Girard[†], *Stanford University*

Andrew McKenna, *Loyola University of Chicago*

Raymund Schwager[†], *University of Innsbruck*

James Williams, *Syracuse University*

EDITORIAL BOARD

Rebecca Adams, *Independent Scholar*

Jeremiah L. Alberg, *International Christian University, Tokyo, Japan*

Mark Anspach, *École des Hautes Études en Sciences Sociales, Paris*

Pierpaolo Antonello, *University of Cambridge*

Ann Astell, *University of Notre Dame*

Cesáreo Bandera, *University of North Carolina*

Maria Stella Barberi, *Università di Messina*

Alexei Bodrov, *St. Andrew's Biblical Theological Institute, Moscow*

João Cezar de Castro Rocha, *Universidade do Estado do Rio de Janeiro*

Benoît Chantre, *L'Association Recherches Mimétiques*

Diana Culbertson, *Kent State University*

Paul Dumouchel, *Université du Québec à Montréal*

Jean-Pierre Dupuy, *Stanford University, École Polytechnique*

Giuseppe Fornari, *Università degli studi di Verona*

Eric Gans, *University of California, Los Angeles*

Sandor Goodhart, *Purdue University*

Robert Hamerton-Kelly[†], *Stanford University*

Hans Jensen, *Aarhus University, Denmark*

Mark Juergensmeyer, *University of California, Santa Barbara*

Grant Kaplan, *Saint Louis University*

Cheryl Kirk-Duggan, *Shaw University*

Michael Kirwan, SJ, *Trinity College Dublin*

Paisley Livingston, *Lingnan University, Hong Kong*

Charles Mabee, *Ecumenical Theological Seminary, Detroit*

Józef Niewiadomski, *Universität Innsbruck*

Wolfgang Palaver, *Universität Innsbruck*

Ángel Jorge Barahona Plaza, *Universidad Francisco de Vitoria*

Petra Steinmair-Pösel, *KPH Edith Stein*

Martha Reineke, *University of Northern Iowa*

Julia Robinson Moore, *University of North Carolina at Charlotte*

Tobin Siebers[†], *University of Michigan*

Thee Smith, *Emory University*

Mark Wallace, *Swarthmore College*

Nikolaus Wandinger, *University of Innsbruck, Austria*

Eugene Webb, *University of Washington*

How to Think About Catastrophe

Toward a Theory of Enlightened Doomsaying

Jean-Pierre Dupuy

Translated by
M. B. DeBevoise and
Mark R. Anspach

Michigan State University Press · *East Lansing*

English translation copyright © 2023 by Michigan State University; *Pour un catastrophisme éclairé: Quand l'impossible est certain* copyright © 2002 by Éditions du Seuil

Michigan State University Press
East Lansing, Michigan 48823-5245

Printed and bound in the United States of America.

27 26 25 24 23 22 21 20 19 18   1 2 3 4 5 6 7 8 9 10

LIBRARY OF CONGRESS CATALOGING-IN-PUBLICATION DATA
Names: Dupuy, Jean-Pierre, 1941– author. | DeBevoise, M. B., translator. | Anspach, Mark Rogin, 1959– translator.
Title: How to think about catastrophe : toward a theory of enlightened doomsaying / Jean-Pierre Dupuy ; translated by M. B. DeBevoise and Mark R. Anspach.
Other titles: Pour un catastrophisme éclairé. English
Description: First. | East Lansing : Michigan State University Press, [2022] | Series: Studies in violence, mimesis, and culture | Includes bibliographical references and index.
Identifiers: LCCN 2021056064 | ISBN 9781611864366 (paperback) | ISBN 9781609177065 (pdf) | ISBN 9781628954746 (epub) | ISBN 9781628964684 (kindle)
Subjects: LCSH: Catastrophical, The
Classification: LCC BD375 D8713 2022 | DDC 133.3—dc23/eng/20211202
LC record available at https://lccn.loc.gov/2021056064

Cover design by David Drummond, Salamander Design, www.salamanderhill.com.
Cover art: Richard Ernest Eurich, *Jonah and the Whale*, c.1980 (oil on canvas, 50.8x61 cms). Photo © Christie's Images / © Estate of Richard Eurich. All rights reserved 2022 / Bridgeman Images.

Visit Michigan State University Press at *www.msupress.org*

So the Platonic Year
Whirls out new right and wrong,
Whirls in the old instead;
All men are dancers and their tread
Goes to the barbarous clangour of a gong.
—W. B. Yeats, *The Tower*

This is the way the world ends
This is the way the world ends
This is the way the world ends
Not with a bang but a whimper
—T. S. Eliot, *The Hollow Men*

Contents

ix Prologue. A Time of Catastrophes

PART ONE | Risk and Fatality

3 CHAPTER 1. A Singular Point of View

13 CHAPTER 2. Sacrifice, Counterproductivity, and Ethics, or the Logic of the Detour

25 CHAPTER 3. Fate, Risk, and Responsibility

37 CHAPTER 4. The Autonomy of Technology

47 CHAPTER 5. Doomsaying on Trial

PART TWO | The Limits of Economic Rationality

63   CHAPTER 6. Precaution, Between Risk and Uncertainty

75   CHAPTER 7. The Veil of Ignorance and Moral Luck

83   CHAPTER 8. Knowing Is Not Believing

PART THREE | The Limits of Moral Philosophy and the Necessity of Metaphysics

97   CHAPTER 9. Memory of the Future

105   CHAPTER 10. Predicting the Future in Order to Change It (Jonah vs. Jonas)

115   CHAPTER 11. Projected Time and Occurring Time

131   CHAPTER 12. The Rationality of Doomsaying

143   NOTES

161   INDEX

PROLOGUE

A Time of Catastrophes

In order to picture to itself an unknown situation the imagination borrows elements that are already familiar and, for that reason, cannot picture it. But the sensibility, even in its most physical form, receives, like the wake of a thunderbolt, the original and for long indelible imprint of the novel event.

—Marcel Proust, *The Fugitive*

This book has its origins in a talk I gave on March 1, 2001, at the French economic planning agency, the Commissariat Général du Plan, as the inaugural lecture of a seminar on new risks facing France and other advanced industrialized societies. Under the circumstances, I might have been expected to strike the managerial tone usually thought to be appropriate to a gathering of business leaders and senior government officials. Out of conviction, however, rather than any desire to shock my listeners, I resolved to adopt the attitude of a doomsayer. The reader will see exactly what I mean by this in the pages that follow. At all events, my remarks stimulated debate. Urged to expand the text of my talk into a book, I drew upon the course of lectures I had prepared for a class at Stanford University that spring elaborating the concept of "enlightened doomsaying." The main part of the task was complete by the end of the summer.

Then came September 11—a date that, like every watershed event in human history, marked off what came before from what came after. An unprecedented catastrophe had suddenly struck. The worst had happened. Until then the catastrophes that I had been thinking about were ones brought about by the limitless extension of human power over the natural world. The catastrophe of September 11 made manifest the extreme violence that human beings are capable of visiting upon one another. Was the difference between the two kinds of disaster really so great? It is not an insignificant detail that the weapons used in this attack were technological objects diverted from their customary purpose, as if the power of human ingenuity had been turned against itself. In France, the explosion of a chemical factory in Toulouse ten days later confused the issue all the more, as politicians and pundits hastened to link the two events. How to protect the country against future terrorist attacks became the top priority. One proposal called for equipping each new nuclear power plant with a battery of surface-to-air missiles, as had already been done at two radioactive-waste processing plants in La Hague—threatening to make overflights of French territory by civilian airliners fraught with danger. A time of catastrophes was now upon us.

The world experienced the events of September 11 less as the inscription into reality of something utterly insane and hence impossible than as the sudden intrusion of the newly possible into the realm of the once-impossible. Before September 11 it was thought that such things could not happen. After September 11, one heard it said, even the worst horrors had become possible. If something *becomes* possible, this means it was not possible before. And yet, common sense objects, if it actually occurs, this must mean it *was* possible all along. This apparent contradiction I have deliberately placed at the heart of an argument that I intend to be both catastrophist and rational. The link between catastrophes of human power over nature and catastrophes of internecine violence, I am now convinced, is located precisely here.

In *The Two Sources of Morality and Religion* (1918), Henri Bergson describes the sensations he felt on August 4, 1914, upon learning of Germany's declaration of war on France:

A Time of Catastrophes

Horror-struck though I was, and though I felt a war, even a victorious war, to be a catastrophe, I experienced what William James expresses, a feeling of admiration for the smoothness of the transition from the abstract to the concrete: who would have thought that so terrible an eventuality could make its entrance into reality with so little fuss? This impression of simplicity was predominant above all else.[1]

Bergson goes on to suggest that creating a sense of familiarity with a cataclysmic event is nature's way of preventing a paralysis of the will. Yet this uncanny familiarity stood in sharp contrast to Bergson's feelings *before* the catastrophe. The prospect of war appeared to him as "*at once probable and impossible*: a complex and contradictory idea that lasted right down to the fateful day."[2]

Some years later, Bergson managed very well to unravel this apparent contradiction when reflecting upon the nature of works of art in an essay entitled "The Possible and the Real" (1930). "I believe in the end we shall consider it evident," Bergson wrote, "that the artist in executing his work *is creating the possible as well as the real*." Why is it, then, he asked, that one might "hesitate to say the same thing for nature? Is not the world a work of art incomparably richer than that of the greatest artist?"[3] The hesitation to extend this idea to acts of destruction is greater still. And yet who has contemplated the images of September 11 and not been filled with a feeling of exaltation and dread that resembles what one feels in the presence of the sublime, in the sense that Burke and Kant gave to this word? Of the terrorists, who could hardly have failed to have sensations of the same kind, we may also say that they created the possible at the same time as they created the real. This was, as I said, the metaphysical view that most people spontaneously adopted, though perhaps without always knowing it. We must therefore follow Bergson's reasoning on this point with great care, for it goes to the very heart of our attitude toward catastrophe.

Bergson reports a delightful conversation with a journalist who had come to interview him, during the Great War, on the subject of the future of literature. "How do you conceive, for example, the great dramatic work of tomorrow?" he was asked.

"But," Bergson objected, "the work of which you speak is not yet possible."

"But it must be, since it will be created," retorted the other.

To this Bergson replied, "No, it is not. I grant you, at most, that it *will have been possible.*"

"What do you mean by that?"

"It's quite simple. Let a man of talent or genius come forth, let him create a work: it will then be real, and by that very fact it becomes retrospectively or retroactively possible. It would not be possible, it would not have been so, if this man had not come upon the scene. That is why I tell you that it will have been possible today, but that it is not yet so."

"You're not serious! You are surely not going to maintain that the future has an effect upon the present, that the present brings something into the past, that action works back over the course of time and imprints its mark afterwards?"

"That depends. That one can put reality into the past and thus work backwards in time is something I have never claimed. But that one can put the possible there, or rather that the possible may put itself there at any moment, is not to be doubted. As reality is created as something unforeseeable and new, its image is reflected behind it into the indefinite past; thus it finds that it has from all time been possible, but it is at this precise moment that it *begins to have always been possible*, and that is why I said that its possibility, which does not precede its reality, will have preceded it once the reality has appeared."[4]

The time of catastrophes embodies this temporality, which, in effect, entangles past and future. A catastrophe, as an event surging forth, suddenly arising out of nothingness, becomes possible in the course of "possibilizing" itself—to speak in the manner of Sartre, who, on this point, had well remembered the lesson of his own teacher, Bergson. The source of our problem is to be found right here. On the one hand, anyone who wishes to *prevent* a catastrophe must believe in its possibility *before* it occurs. On the other hand, if one succeeds in actually preventing it, its non-realization keeps it firmly within the realm of the impossible, and efforts at prevention appear in retrospect to have been useless: there was no need to get excited; the peril did not exist.[5]

The urgency of the present moment is, I believe, conceptual, before being political or ethical. That is why I venture to propose a new way of thinking about the future.

·   ·   ·

The present work, as I noted, is an extensively revised and augmented version of the talk I gave in March 2001 at a seminar on emerging risks organized by the French Planning Agency in collaboration with the Ministry of Territorial Development and the Environment, and the Forecasting Division of the Ministry of the Economy, Finance, and Industry. My thanks go first of all to the head of the Commissariat Général du Plan, Jean-Michel Charpin, and to the organizer of the seminar, Michel Matheu, who themselves ran a not inconsiderable risk in inviting a philosopher to crash the discussions among technocrats. My talk aroused many reactions, some hostile, others sympathetic without being uncritical. I have profited from all of them, beginning with the response of two eminent figures in the scientific world who were asked to comment on my remarks, the biologist Jacques Testart and the professor of medicine Didier Sicard, the then-chair of the French Ethics Committee for the Life Sciences. I owe thanks, too, to François Ewald, Olivier Godard, Georges-Yves Kervern, Catherine Larrère, Raphaël Larrère, Christian Gollier, Grégoire Postel-Vinay, and Bernard Guibert, as well as to my students at Stanford and at the École Polytechnique in Paris, where I presented my ideas at various sessions of the seminar on moral philosophy that Monique Canto-Sperber and I taught together. The comments of Jon Elster, Pierre Livet, Jean Petitot, Philippe Nemo, Philippe Mongin, Michel Horps, Rodolf Greif, Peter Railton, Lucien Scubla, Mark Anspach, Michel Bitbol, Michel De Glas, Pierre Saurel, Simon Charbonneau, Olivier Cuny, Aviv Bergman, Alexei Grinbaum, François Velde, Michel Petit, and Ruwen Ogien have been no less valuable to me. I am pleased to acknowledge my debt to all of these friends and colleagues, and most especially to Monique Canto-Sperber, who carefully reread the final manuscript and who has been a constant source of support and encouragement.

It goes without saying that responsibility for the views I express in this book is nevertheless mine alone. I have striven to refine highly technical concepts as precisely as possible in order to further reflection on a subject that ordinarily inspires impassioned reactions since what is at issue is nothing less than the survival of the human race. Some readers may find the mixture of philosophical analysis and apocalyptic prophecy surprising. So be it. I have been guided solely by the conviction that from now on we must learn to think in the shadow of future catastrophe.

PART ONE

Risk and Fatality

CHAPTER 1

A Singular Point of View

François Guery: What makes you think that the danger is
extremely serious?

Corinne Lepage: I don't know if the danger is extremely
serious or not—and that is precisely the problem.

—Guery and Lepage discussing genetically modified
organisms in their book *La politique de précaution*

During the last century humanity acquired the ability to destroy itself,
either directly, through nuclear war, or indirectly, by altering the conditions necessary to its survival. The breach of this fateful threshold had
been a long time in the making, but now what had seemed only a remote danger was made acute and plain for all to see. Today the recurrent crises involving
the environment resemble those more or less serious ailments that are apt to
seem more disturbing than they really are to the extent that they remind us of
our mortality. Nature transcended itself in bringing forth the human race, but
it took an enormous risk in doing so. As if to hedge against this risk, it endowed
humans with a spiritual faculty, the spark of practical wisdom known as ethics.

Only by making good use of this faculty can humanity hope to curb its
power over things and over itself—a power that is excessive and, above all,

destructive. Industrial society, which depends on the continuing advance of science and technology, seems now to have discovered—with what agitation and confusion!—that exceedingly serious threats weigh on its future. The term conventionally used to designate the object of this new awareness is "risk." I shall try to show that the word is very poorly chosen.

The question of risk can be approached from various points of view. No branch of the social sciences has a deeper acquaintance with this topic than economics. Even before the advent of economics as an independent discipline, the theory of decision-making under uncertainty had come into being in the work of the most eminent mathematicians of the seventeenth century. Thanks to the calculus of probabilities pioneered by Pascal, Fermat, and Huygens, games of chance were now subject to the laws of human reason. In the twentieth century, the mathematicians John von Neumann and Leonard Savage sought to place economics on more secure foundations by working out a theory of rational choice. It is significant that, in looking to axiomatize the assumptions that they held to define rationality, von Neumann and Savage had begun by considering the case of a person faced with an uncertain future—someone, say, who decides to try their luck in a lottery and estimates the respective probabilities of winning different prizes. Even today, experts who seek to evaluate threats to the environment or human health adopt the same framework of analysis. When one of them warns that "humanity is in trouble: up to 10,000 people die daily because of avoidable environmental foreclosure in their wretched lives. . . . [We are taking] a huge gamble with [the earth's] future climate,"[1] it is clear that he cannot free himself from the hold of Pascal's metaphor of games of chance. Will the victims of environmental disasters shrug and say that they have simply drawn an unlucky number in a lottery? No, they will rebel against what they see as an unjust outcome, an incomprehensible twist of fate for which they feel they are not in the least responsible.

And yet in the many research centers and think tanks where questions of the environment and public health are studied, economists—or in any case the spirit of their discipline—dominate the debate. The idea of insurance also has a prominent place in their thinking, for if one supposes that threats assume the same form as the risk one takes in betting on a random event, such as the result of a football game or a horse race, then they are insurable. But the next major terrorist attack can no more be insured against than the explosion of a nuclear reactor on the river Seine upstream of Paris. Thinking about environmental dangers has nevertheless been reduced for the most part to an exercise in environmental economics. There are strong reasons to fear that this quasi-monopoly may have very harmful consequences. It will suffice for the moment to sketch two of them. In the first place, economists readily acknowledge that they are not capable of meeting the challenge alone, and that the ethical and political dimensions of the problems they address cannot be neglected. Nevertheless they hold that their approach is *separable* from this larger moral context, and that they can therefore carry out their calculations of risk in isolation from all other considerations. I shall argue, against this view, that the search for an ethics appropriate to our present situation must call into question the philosophical foundations of economic calculus.

A second motivation for resisting the dominance of economic thought in the approach to risks (through reliance on cost-benefit analysis, for example) is that economic thinking is itself at the origin of the risks it presumes to judge. Reading the many published commentaries on our "risk society," one is often overcome by a sense of unreality, so completely has the context of the threats identified with risks been erased. As if the invasion of the world by commercial values, the tendency to regard all human activity as a function of production and consumption, really had nothing to do with the dangers facing us! As if economic thinking were not in fact profoundly implicated in the vast movement of globalization and the runaway engine of growth that condition its existence while escaping its grasp . . .

Economics is not the only branch of social science to concern itself with such questions, of course. The social psychology of collective phenomena; the political and socioeconomic aspects of regulatory policy; the relations between science, technology, and society; the logic of legal liability; the political and administrative role of government in managing risk and crises—these are only a few of the topics that claim the attention of neighboring disciplines as they attempt to advance the widely shared aim of drawing up a charter of technological democracy that would dramatically redefine the respective roles of scientists, scholars, the state, and civil society. These efforts are perfectly legitimate, and sometimes yield works of high quality. In giving priority to political considerations over economic calculation, they proceed from the conviction that, so long as momentous decisions concerning scientific and technological development are taken without consulting the wishes of a well-informed populace, any precautionary policy that may be adopted will produce effects opposite to the ones it was meant to produce, causing panic rather than calming tensions, and making extreme reactions more rather than less likely. However worthy, such reflections strike me as premature. They put the cart before the horse. Before devising political procedures that could allow a scientific and technological democracy to travel along whichever road it chooses, or in any case to avoid the highways that will swiftly lead straight to disaster, we must first be sure we understand the nature of the ills we are seeking to avert.

In the course of recent decades, the idea has taken root, especially in France, that collective rationality can be conceived only in procedural terms, and that democracy is first and foremost a matter of constructing a public space for communication and deliberation. To say that rationality is procedural is to say that once agreement has been reached regarding the procedures that will be implemented, then what follows from them will ipso facto be just and good. This amounts to renouncing the search, independently of and prior to any procedure, for the criteria of the just and the good, or rather, as we shall see, of unacceptable harm and injury. Procedural rationality is all very fine, except when it comes at the price of renouncing substantive rationality.[2] In relation to the major problems facing humanity—uncontrolled technological innovation, reliance on arms of mass destruction to achieve deterrence, rampant environmental degradation—too often the appeal to democratic procedures serves as an excuse for the absence of normative reflection.

Paradoxically, the sociopolitical approach to the issue of risk often generates works that look even more unreal than the writings of economists, who have never concealed their fondness for unrealistic abstractions. To take an illustration that will occupy us throughout this book, what does such a sociological perspective have to tell us about the origins of the uncertainty surrounding the prospect of catastrophe? It is not known, for example, whether the warming climate produced by gases already present in the upper atmosphere will lead over the course of a few centuries to an increase in temperature of less than two degrees Celsius or of more than seven degrees compared to the pre-industrial era. The difference in environmental impact associated with these two estimates is roughly the difference between a scratch on the chin and a mortal blow to the skull. What accounts for such a difference? The orthodox answer in some quarters is that it is due to scientific controversy, the outcome of which, in the revisionist view of some sociologists and historians of science, depends solely on institutional relations of force and power. On this view, science is a battlefield where the standard-bearers of a given "paradigm" seek to win prestige and capture control over academic appointments and research funding. Scientific uncertainty is therefore seen to resemble the glorious uncertainty of sports, where the best team may lose if the element of chance inherent in any competition nullifies its presumptive advantage—except that in this vision of science, the notion of "best team" loses all meaning. Certainly there is nothing in the least ingenuous about this way of looking at the matter. Nevertheless a basic question remains that does not even occur to the revisionists: preoccupied with deconstructing the image of science as an enterprise that rationally and methodically advances from one discovery to the next, they fail to ask themselves how anything like the objectivity and practical effectiveness that indisputably characterize science and technology could emerge from the violent free-for-all that they see in them.

There is a curious reversal at work in all of this. No longer are the intrinsic properties of an object, for instance its complexity, held to be responsible for scientific controversy, by rendering knowledge irreducibly uncertain; instead it is the controversy itself that is said to be responsible for the uncertainty.

The quite different *philosophical* inquiry that I am undertaking presupposes that one must understand the world before setting about to change it. The world seems perfectly willing to take on the job of transformation without our help! What is needed in the first place is a theory that explains the etiology of the dangers we face, and why the sky suddenly seems poised to fall on our heads. As François Guery put it, "We are dumbfounded to discover that unprecedented consequences appear as if out of nowhere, without our being able to anticipate them."[3] More than thirty years ago Jean-Marie Domenach spoke of the "return of the tragic" to the modern world.[4] The managerial perspective that regards the new dangers confronting mankind purely as risks—as though they were at bottom no different from the natural accidents that have always been the lot of human societies—is striking above all for its naiveté, oblivious as it is to the role of the managerial approach itself in the emergence of those same dangers.

I should like to say at the outset that my own approach is intimately linked to my intellectual journey, which led me from the study of mathematics and physics at the École Polytechnique and of economics at the École des Mines to a radical critique of industrial society, and from this critique to a deepening engagement with philosophical questions. The great philosopher of science Jean Ullmo, my mentor at the École Polytechnique, with whose encouragement and support I later established that institution's first center of philosophical research, was fond of calling me a "rationalist extremist"—an epithet that I do not disavow. Indeed, it explains my determination in the pages that follow to argue on behalf of a rational and enlightened form of "doomsaying."

Early in my career, in the 1970s, I helped to introduce the thought of Ivan Illich to French readers.[5] At the time a number of us were already foretelling in broad strokes the immense panic that seems to loom just beyond our immediate horizon—prophets of doom, as we were called. Here again I freely admit to sharing this attitude, which I shall try to justify with rational arguments. For the moment let me briefly summarize the thrust of Illich's critique, and in particular the concept of counterproductivity, before going on to examine it in greater detail.

Every use value can be produced in two ways. These correspond to two modes of production, the one *autonomous* and the other *heteronomous*. Learning, for example, may take place spontaneously in a setting that stimulates the imagination; one may also choose to receive instruction from a teacher who is paid for this purpose. One can keep oneself in good health by leading an active, wholesome life; one may also be treated by a health professional. One may have a relationship to the space one inhabits that grows out of the use of low-speed forms of locomotion such as walking or bicycling; one may also have an instrumental relationship to this space, with the aim of passing through it—of being done with it—as quickly as possible, by using motorized transport. One may render *service* to someone who asks you for assistance; one may also say: there are *services* for that.

Unlike the products of heteronomous activity, what the autonomous mode produces cannot in general be measured, evaluated, compared with, or added to other values. The use values yielded by this mode therefore elude the grasp of the economist, which is why they do not figure in reckonings of gross national product. This, of course, is not to say that the heteronomous

A Singular Point of View

9

mode is intrinsically harmful—far from it. But the great question that Illich had the merit of posing has to do with the manner in which the two modes are related to each other. It is not a matter of denying that heteronomous production can dramatically increase people's autonomy in the production of use values. In the best cases, schools enhance pupils' capacity to learn on their own and doctors help patients to stay in good health. But here heteronomy is only a *detour*, a provisional *turning away* from production in order to bring about a greater autonomy. What Illich called "positive synergy" between the two modes of production is possible only under a set of very precise conditions. Beyond certain critical *thresholds* of development, heteronomous production leads to a complete reorganization of the physical, institutional, and symbolic environment of a society, with the result that autonomous capacities are paralyzed. This in turn sets in motion a vicious circle, which Illich called *counterproductivity*. With the impoverishment of those experiences that put a person in direct contact with others, and with the world around him, there arises a powerful demand for heteronomous substitutes that make it possible to endure life in an increasingly alienating world while at the same time reinforcing the conditions that make them necessary. This in turn yields the paradoxical result that, beyond certain critical thresholds, the more widespread heteronomous production becomes, the more it becomes an obstacle to the realization of the very purposes that it is supposed to serve. Thus medicine undermines health, education dulls the mind, transportation immobilizes, communication systems make us deaf and dumb, information destroys meaning, and fossil fuels, which revive the dynamism of past life, threaten to extinguish the possibility of life in the future. Last, but not least, industrial processing transforms food into poison.

Illich believed that this runaway phenomenon of self-*de*regulation, this uncontrollable chain reaction, could best be expressed in religious terms: we are guilty of hubris, and jealous divinities have sent the goddess of vengeance, Nemesis, to punish us.[6] Elsewhere I have told how my trip to Cuernavaca, in Mexico, where Illich lived and worked, led me from the rational to the irrational and from the irrational to reason. It was in Cuernavaca that I got to know Heinz von Foerster, a pioneer of cybernetics and one of the founders of cognitive science. Through the cunning of personal history, this encounter led me to become one of the architects of cognitive science in France, while at the same time maintaining a critical distance from it that became still more pronounced as the years went by.[7] Nevertheless I wish to emphasize that my approach does not in any way constitute a critique of modern reason, for my thinking is wholly informed by science and technology. Some of the greatest joys of my life I owe to the practice of science. From an early age mathematical imagination took the place of poetry for me. As for technology, I consider it less an unavoidable instrument than a cause for wonder and reflection. This is something that Heidegger and his followers did not understand: "contemplative" thought can hope to find no more suitable object than the masterpieces of "calculating" thought embodied today by neural networks in the field of artificial intelligence and tomorrow by the quantum computers that will revolutionize our conceptions of the natural and the artificial.

What I wish to criticize, then, is not technology itself, but the technological project that animates industrial society. By this I mean the determination to replace the social fabric, the bonds of solidarity that constitute the weft and warp of a society, with a fabrication; the unprecedented enterprise of manufacturing relationships with one's neighbors and the world in the same way as one manufactures automobiles or fiberglass. The freeway, the artificial kidney, and the internet are not only technological objects or systems; they betray a peculiar sort of instrumental relationship to space, to death, and to meaning. It is this instrumental relationship and the underlying dream of mastery that critics need to scrutinize. For in seeking to dominate nature and history through the tools they have made, human beings must not let themselves become slaves to these very same tools. The technological project is not neutral: contrary to conventional wisdom on both the right and the left, it does not produce good or evil depending on the intentions of those who manage it. At the very moment that Illich's critique was gaining an audience in France, the mayor of Paris was promising to build "convivial" freeways and the French Communists were promising that with the realization of their program, people would spend twice as much time traveling by public transport as under capitalist austerity. None of them was able to prevent a society built around freeways and high-speed trains from erecting more barriers among its citizens than it tore down.

Criticizing "modernity" makes no more sense than criticizing a tsunami or a hurricane. Like Tocqueville, we may say that the onward march of modernity is "a providential fact": "it is universal, it is lasting, and it constantly eludes human interference"; it "is served equally by every event and every human being." Indeed, Tocqueville emphasized, "all men have helped its progress with their efforts," both "those who fought on its behalf and those who were its declared opponents."[8] Even such a "doomsayer" as Hans Jonas, to whom we shall return later, concurs in this view. "In this whole context," Jonas remarks, modern technological prowess "plays a complex and partly paradoxical role. The source of the dreaded misfortune, it may at the same time be the only way to forestall the latter, for doing so requires the unrestrained application of the very knowledge from which the fatal power springs."[9] A no less paradoxical lesson of the tragedy of September 11, 2001, is that the most radical challenges to modernity, which reject the democratic path of criticism in favor of the nihilistic path of destruction, can succeed in their criminal purpose only by casting themselves in the mold of modernity and exploiting fully the technological instruments of its prowess.

The model of scientific, technological, economic, and political development pursued by advanced industrial societies nonetheless suffers from a crippling contradiction. In taking its values and institutions to be universal, the modern mind does not pause to consider that this might in fact not be the case; indeed, in its most autistic fantasies it believes that human history could not have *not* led to modernity. Modernity imagines itself to constitute the end of history—an end that in a sense redeems all the achingly laborious processes of trial and error that preceded it and that, by virtue of just this, gives them meaning. And yet modern societies have at the same time come to realize that universalizing their model of development will inevitably run up against formidable obstacles given the limited capacity of the earth to sustain such development.

We must therefore decide what we consider more essential: the ethical requirement of equality, which presupposes principles that can be universalized, or else the mode of development we have embraced until now. One cannot have it both ways. Either the developed world must increasingly isolate itself behind all kinds of protective barriers to thwart ever more cruel assaults born of the resentment of those it excludes; or else we need to invent another way of relating to the world, and to nature, to inanimate things and living creatures, that will lend itself to being universalized to all humanity.

CHAPTER TWO

Sacrifice, Counterproductivity, and Ethics, or the Logic of the Detour

The horror, the horror.
—Joseph Conrad, *Heart of Darkness*

The social critique of capitalism and, beyond that, of industrial society has often taken aim at instrumental rationality, or rather at the monopoly that this form of rationality has enjoyed over human reason in modern society. From the imperialism of instrumental rationality, it is held, there arose what Max Weber called the "disenchantment of the world," which is to say the instrumentalization of nature and the reduction of every living creature and every inanimate thing to the status of a simple means in the service of an end that goes beyond them. The revolt against instrumental rationality may be found in styles of thought as varied as Marxism, the Heideggerian critique of technology, the philosophy and sociology of the Frankfurt School, postmodern theory and deconstruction, and the radical version of environmentalism known as political ecology. All of them, I believe, take aim at the wrong target.

A more powerful and more original analysis can be found in the writings of Ivan Illich. The crucial feature of industrialization in his view is not its relations of production, as the Marxist characterization of capitalism would have it, or even a certain type of technological relationship to nature. Instead, the fundamental trait is what I call the *logic of the detour*. This logic, in turn, is rooted in religion.

The work of a leading contemporary theorist of rational choice, Jon Elster, may be taken as a point of departure.[1] Elster draws our attention to the elective affinities that link capitalism with the philosophical system of Leibniz. Like the author of the *Theodicy*, he argues that human beings are characterized by their ability to take a roundabout route when this will help them to attain their ends more efficiently. They are able to take a detour to reach their destination more quickly, to temporarily refrain from consuming and to invest in order to increase their overall consumption, to refuse a favorable opportunity in order to wait for a still more favorable one, and so on. Ethologists regard this capacity, which is intimately bound up with instrumental rationality, as the defining characteristic of intelligence.

The philosophy of action implicit in neoclassical economic theory is consistent with this argument, since it holds that acting rationally consists in maximizing a certain magnitude. Elster insists that this maximization principle must be understood as implying a *global* maximization rather than a merely local one. Suppose that we are standing on a mountain top and a higher peak is visible in the distance. If we are not content with local maximization, we must be willing to climb back down from our present elevation before ascending to a greater height. To think otherwise would amount to committing what is known as the "first-step fallacy." Someone who blasts off to the moon and lands instead in a tree must resign himself to coming back down to earth in order to devise a more effective technique of rocket propulsion.

Elster suggests that what we call reason in this case is wholly informed by religion and ethics. Like many other authors,[2] he has rightly sought the sources of modern rationalism in Leibniz's *Theodicy* (1710) and *Monadology* (1714). Seeing man as that singular being who is capable of stepping back in order to leap forward, Leibniz takes him to be a faithful image of his Creator. In order to bring into existence the best of all possible worlds—the best remaining imperfect, for perfection is an attribute of God, not of His creation—God had to allow some small measure of evil to subsist, for otherwise the world would have been, everything considered, still worse. Everything that appears to be evil from the finite point of view of the individual monad is, from the point of view of the totality, a sacrifice necessary for the greater good of the whole. Evil is always sacrificial in this sense, and sacrifice may be thought of in turn as a detour. Louis Dumont characterizes the logical form of theodicy by means of the following formula: "Good must contain evil while still being its contrary."[3] Here the word *contain* has the sense of "encompass," and the paradoxical form thus described is what Dumont calls "hierarchy"—a term he uses in its etymological sense of "sacred order" and defines as the "encompassing of the contrary." Elsewhere I have shown that if the word *contain* is understood in its dual sense of encompassing *and* of keeping in check, or holding back, theodicy displays the same form as Adam Smith's "invisible hand."[4]

Instrumental rationality, the justification of evil, and economic logic are all closely associated with one another and jointly constitute the matrix, or womb, of modern reason. Economic rationality is first of all a moral economy, for it involves the rational management of sacrifice. Sacrifice is a "production cost"—the detour that must be made in order to maximize the *summum bonum* or "highest good."[5]

I shall defend the following thesis. The logic of the detour constitutes a key element of modern ideology[6] and lies at the heart of economic rationality. However, if we leave behind our illusory self-representations, we shall discover two things: first, that the ability to make detours, far from being an essential property of what it means to be human, is denied to us in fundamental areas of our lives, or else can be exercised only with great difficulty; second, that this ability, when it is present, far from constituting an "adaptive advantage"[7] may actually serve to hinder or thwart the aims of instrumental rationality, which is wrongly thought always to act in concert with it.

More precisely: firstly, the logic of the detour, as an ethical proposition, is repugnant to the inhabitants of modern societies; secondly, as Illich has demonstrated, it can be counterproductive in the highest degree. I shall deal with this last point first, before coming to the ethical question.

Illich's critique is aimed not at the logic of the detour as such, but at the hold it has over our minds. We are apt to lose sight of the fact that a detour is just that, a detour, and nothing more. Someone who steps back in order to leap forward keeps his eyes fixed on the obstacle that he is trying to overcome. If he steps back while looking in the opposite direction, there is a chance that he will forget his original objective and, mistaking his regress for progress, confuse the means with the ends. Rationality is then converted into counterproductivity; it takes the form of the torment of Tantalus. What enables us to recognize this tragic reversal is none other than the requirement that means be optimally adapted to their ends, which is to say instrumental rationality itself. We therefore cannot blame instrumental rationality for this reversal.

In the 1970s I worked with Illich on an argument of this type, the point of which was to bring out the counterproductivity of the major institutions of modern society: school, medicine, transportation, and so on.[8] As we mounted our radical challenge to conventional thinking, we did not hesitate to subject those institutions to mockery, which at the time was an effective weapon. It misfires today, since a society that trembles for the future of its children can no longer laugh at its own lethal shortcomings. It will be instructive to examine one particular component of our critique that perfectly illustrates the point I have just made, namely, that the willingness to make detours can become the enemy of instrumental rationality. Together with a team of researchers I carried out a series of offbeat but rigorous calculations[9] that yielded the following result: the average Frenchman devoted more than four hours a day to his car, driving it from one place to another, cleaning and taking care of it, and, most importantly, working in a factory or office in order to make enough money to pay for the car's purchase, use, and maintenance. Recently I went back over the data we had analyzed and came to the conclusion that the present situation is doubtless worse than it was twenty years ago.[10]

Dividing the average number of kilometers traveled on all types of trip by the total amount of time devoted to the car (or "generalized time," as we called it), one obtains an estimate of the "generalized" speed, which turned out to be roughly seven kilometers (or four miles) per hour—somewhat faster than a person walking at a normal pace, but considerably slower than riding a bicycle.[11] As unusual as this calculation may seem, it is nevertheless modeled on the ones that transportation economists make in comparing, for example, the net advantages of two modes of transport. What they do in such cases is work out the respective generalized costs by assigning a monetary value to time, usually based on the hourly wage. The generalized time that we calculated is identical to the transportation economist's generalized cost divided by the time value. Instead of converting investments of time into monetary units, we converted costs into units of time.

In *arithmetic* terms, the result we obtained means that the average French person, separated from their car—and therefore, let us assume, freed from the necessity of working long hours in order to pay for it—would spend less generalized time getting from here to there by traveling everywhere on a bicycle. This includes *all* trips: not only ones made during the week as part of the daily commute between home and work, but also weekend outings in the countryside and holiday excursions to more distant seashore resorts. This "alternative" scenario would unanimously be deemed unthinkable and absurd. And yet traveling by bicycle would save time, energy, and scarce resources and be far kinder to the environment. What is it, then, that makes the one situation preposterous on its face, whereas the risibility of the other situation cannot be seen? Is it really less comical to work a large part of every day simply to be able to afford to go to work?

The preceding calculation assumes the equivalence between one hour of transportation and one hour of work, each one being considered a means in the service of another end. The very same equivalence inspires the calculations of the transportation economist. One may question this equivalence, but it must be acknowledged that it is only a consequence of taking seriously the logic of the detour. Neither labor nor transportation is an end in itself. The purpose of economic calculus is to quantify as accurately as possible the pains to which people go to attain a given output so that the sum total can be kept to a minimum. As their etymology reveals, both *travel* and labor (provided one says it in French: *travail*) are sources of pains and torments. The two words, "travel" and *travail*, are what linguists call doublets, both descended from *tripalium*, the Latin name for a three-pronged medieval instrument of torture.

In truth, if the absurdity is hidden from us of a way of life and a structuring of social space and time that leads so many people to devote so much generalized time to getting from place to place, and, on average, with so little efficiency, this is because they substitute work time for travel time. In principle—the principle that we called the logic of the detour—their labor is only a means for achieving more rapid and efficient transportation, which in its turn is only a means for attaining some other end (for example, "bringing loved ones closer together," to quote the advertising slogan of a French automaker). In keeping with the logic of the detour (and in a way that discloses its ideological character), our calculation showed that the time spent in designing and building powerful machines meant to help us save time more than cancels out the time that they actually save. The hare feverishly rushes about office suites and assembly lines, but, as in La Fontaine's fable, it is the tortoise that finishes first. Alas, the tortoise is an endangered species. So much for the ingenuous notion that the economy is designed to "economize" human toil and drudgery! It should be obvious by now that everything is arranged as though the objective were to keep people perpetually busy—even if it means making them run in place faster and faster.

No more elaborate detour can be imagined than the division of labor one finds in present-day economies. There are people who work at producing lethal weapons, for example, in exchange for the money they need to pay for expensive medical services—and this in order to bring about a result, namely, good health, that they could have achieved in large measure themselves by leading a healthier life. The spirit of the detour has been so thoroughly perverted by industrial society and its highly developed division of labor that the detour itself, with all the expenditure of time and energy that it entails, has become an objective pursued for its own sake. That is why our calculation of the automobile's generalized speed was so disturbing: it treated work as an *input*, whereas work in the form of wage labor has become the supreme example of an *output*. Once again, the only people who ought to take this calculation seriously are professional economists. Types of production that are generally agreed to be unnecessary, or even harmful, are routinely justified by the number of jobs they are expected to create. The planned obsolescence of products and appliances, the squandering of non-renewable natural resources, the needless consumption of energy, and the reckless polluting of the environment are all hard to oppose because they provide work. When we made our calculation, a Communist labor union in France was vehemently defending the Concorde program. No one supposed for a moment that the union sought to hasten the advent of a classless society in which former proletarians would travel by supersonic transport. It was fighting to protect jobs. At about the same time another labor union advocated reducing social inequalities on the ground that it would increase consumption by workers and so, by stimulating growth, create more work. Did this amount to confusing the end with the means? No, the ultimate aim of industrial society is to push the logic of the detour to its extreme limit by generating as much work as possible.

Sacrifice, Counterproductivity, and Ethics, or the Logic of the Detour 19

If the capacity for making detours is the distinctive mark of intelligence, then industrial society has made itself stupid from a surfeit of intelligence— stupid enough, as it may well turn out, to bring about its own demise. That in any case is what I held to be true some thirty years ago, when I was collaborating with Illich. Today I would be more circumspect. It seems to me that the collective folly we call economic growth has a "providential" dimension, in Tocqueville's sense—as if the violent and even ruinous transformation of our planet into a single world manifested a purpose that remains a profound mystery. But there is one point on which my spirit of rebellion has not weakened. That the technocrats who pretend to govern us, whether by means of a suavely pedagogical paternalism or a peremptory assertion of authority, try to pass off as dictates of Reason what is only the tragicomic height of the absurd—this is too much for a rationalist of the sort that in spite of everything I remain to this day.

I now come to the question of ethics. The ethics that I have in mind is what might be called our common-sense ethics, anchored in the religious and philosophical traditions of our culture. The intuitions from which it springs are in large measure *deontological*, in the sense that they are cast in the form of absolute prohibitions and obligations that must be respected, whatever the cost for oneself and others. This viewpoint holds, following Rousseau and Kant, that the highest moral faculty, autonomy, consists in limiting one's own individuality by giving oneself an impartial rule or law, transcendent and fixed, and then abiding by it. Common-sense morality is also a morality of intentions that reckons the value of an act by its conformity to norms, rather than by its consequences.

An ethics of this kind will be at odds with any moral doctrine that is consistent with the logic of the detour. Here one thinks of so-called *consequentialist* doctrines, the utilitarian variant of which is closely related to the style of thought found in economics. Consequentialism demands that each person act always in such a way as to contribute to the maximization of an aggregate value that incorporates all of the relevant interests in any particular case, independently of the identity of the persons whose interests these are.[12] Like economic rationality, consequentialist rationality is therefore an instrumental rationality: means are justified by their ends. To be sure, consequentialist rationality embodies an ideal of impartiality that is foreign to economic rationality. The point I am concerned with here, however, is not the relationship between economics and ethics as such, but the fact that an ethical doctrine that satisfies the principle of maximization comes directly into conflict with our most deep-seated moral convictions.[13]

Among these are the conviction that murder is wrong, as are lying and the failure to keep one's promises. Ordinary morality erects on these beliefs a system of prohibitions and obligations that require unswerving obedience from each person: thou shalt not kill, thou shalt honor thy word, and so on. Consequentialism, however, asserts that if it is wrong to kill another person, and if it is right to keep one's promises, the world will be better to the extent that a smaller number of people commit murders and a greater number keep their promises. As a maximizing form of rationality, consequentialism insists on the obligation to promote desirable outcomes as far as possible. This requirement, in and of itself, is not moral, being prior to and independent of any morality. Grafted onto our intuitive convictions concerning right and wrong, however, it yields the categorical imperative of consequentialism: act always in such a way as to increase the *overall* good in the world, and to reduce the *overall* evil.[14]

Now, it so happens that in exceptional cases posing especially thorny ethical dilemmas, the aim of overall maximization can be attained only by transgressing the prohibitions and obligations of common-sense morality. From the consequentialist standpoint, the latter therefore finds itself in the paradoxical position of having to reject absolutely something that would minimize evil and maximize good in overall terms—and all in the name of prohibitions and obligations whose sole justification is that they serve to prevent the same evil and to promote the same good. Traditional morality is founded on the commandment "Thou shalt not kill." Very well—but what if by killing an innocent person, I prevent twenty-two other innocent persons from being killed? If I truly consider the murder of an innocent person to be an abomination, then the prohibition that falls upon murder appears in this case to be contrary to reason. Traditional morality—Christian, Kantian, deontological morality—therefore seems to be guilty of irrationalism: it refuses to step back in order to leap forward; it does not accept the logic of sacrifice; it rejects the principle of the detour.

Critics of utilitarianism who seek to debunk it frequently resort to cases of the type imagined by Robert Nozick: "A mob rampaging through a part of town killing and burning *will* violate the rights of those living there.

Therefore, someone might try to justify his punishing another *he* knows to be innocent of a crime that enraged a mob, on the grounds that punishing this innocent person would help to avoid even greater violations of rights by others, and so would lead to a minimum weighted score for rights violations in the society."[15] The argument seems to be that, since nothing horrifies us more than the prospect of offering up an innocent person to the fury of a mob, utilitarianism, which justifies such an act, must be condemned. But does this mean that the most basic principles of reason must be condemned as well? The situation Nozick describes is none other than the choice framed by Caiaphas, who appealed to the pure reason of the high priests and the Pharisees (John 11:49–50) when he reproached them with the words: "*You understand nothing*, nor do you consider that it is expedient for us that one man should die for the people, and not that the whole nation should perish."

Plainly the words of Caiaphas are not enough to persuade us to reject common-sense morality. The fundamental incompatibility between deontological and consequentialist ethics grows out of their irreconcilable disagreement over the rationality of the detour, which in this case takes the form of a sacrifice. Once again it is to religion that we must look for the source of this rift. In truth, Leibniz's God stands poles apart from the one whose voice is heard in the Gospels. In Luke (15:4–7) Jesus asks, "What man of you, having a hundred sheep, if he loses one of them, does not leave the ninety-nine in the wilderness, and go after the one which is lost until he finds it?" This teaching is fundamentally anti-economistic in spirit since it stands the logic of sacrifice on its head.[16] The wilderness is the place in Hebrew tradition where the scapegoat is abandoned to the demon Azazel so that the community may live.[17] I suspect that the Gospel lesson is largely responsible for the extreme revulsion that common-sense morality feels toward the principle of the detour.

The conflict between the maximizing (and therefore sacrificial) logic of economics and common-sense morality (which, at least under certain circumstances, rejects the sacrificial detour) holds the key to a widely noticed paradox. Modern societies enjoy, it is said, a degree of security unequaled in history, and yet they increasingly perceive themselves to be what the sociologist Ulrich Beck calls "risk societies."[18] Their sensitivity to harm and misfortune is judged out of all proportion to the objective threats to their well-being. "Subjective impressions" are seemingly disconnected from the reasoned, scientific evaluation of risks. It is but a small step to conclude from this, as technocratic elites are sometimes prone to do, that such a degree of sensitivity to risk is irrational and that the gap between subjective perceptions and objective realities must be reduced by educating the public in matters of science and technology. Amateur psychology of this sort is unpersuasive, however. We need to situate the analysis at another level.

The many people in wealthy societies today who find the chief means of access to social recognition closed to them because they cannot find work; who are refused what even primitive societies were able to provide for their poorest members in the way of shelter; who dream of becoming an artist, poet, or musician, or an engineer or computer scientist, and who will never have the chance to cultivate their talents for want of the necessary training— all these marginalized persons are treated as outcasts. But have they *at least* been cast out, excluded from society, *for* a reason? The essence of the difficulty lies in the words that I have emphasized here: "at least" and "for." Let us consider them in turn.

The "at least" makes us shudder today, but it was not always thus. The idea that particular evils may serve a universal good, far from amounting to an extenuating circumstance, now only aggravates the horror of the situation for us. In the 1970s, in a book called *Pyramids of Sacrifice*,[19] the sociologist Peter Berger studied the modern political ideologies that had been used to justify generalized servitude and mass destruction in the name of a radiant future. The title Berger gave to his work suggested that these depraved masterpieces of instrumental rationality—of the belief that the end justifies the means—were remote descendants of the atrocities committed at Tenochtitlán and elsewhere in the name of a bloodthirsty divinity. Kant had already found it inconceivable that the march of human progress should resemble the construction of an edifice that only the last generation could inhabit. The triumph of *homo faber* in human affairs, magisterially analyzed by Hannah Arendt, has now become intolerable.

Do the social marginalization and poverty produced by economic wealth come under the heading of the logic of ends and means? Or, to use Peter Berger's terms, are the marginalized sacrificial victims? Like Berger, I use the word "sacrifice" as a metaphor of its religious sense, returning to the definition given by Hubert and Mauss: in sacrifice, communication with a higher being is established through the mediation of a victim.[20] If exclusion is explained as resulting from *theft*, as one sometimes finds in the Marxist vulgate, this condition is obviously not satisfied: some persons have less *so that* others may have more, but the only higher being is the narrow self-interest of those who come out ahead. The same conclusion follows if the excluded are held to have gotten what they deserve, as a certain neoliberal vulgate would have it.

The great tradition of liberal thought inspired by economics that runs from Adam Smith to Friedrich von Hayek has not hesitated to interpret the harms wrought by the market as sacrifices that must be countenanced in the name of a higher good. In Hayek's portrayal of the market, for example, suffering is rampant: people lack work or lose their jobs, businesses fail, suppliers are abandoned by long-standing customers, speculators take big risks and lose everything, new products find no buyers, fresh discoveries elude the best efforts of researchers, and so on. These penalties are meted out like strokes of fate—unjustified, unpredictable, incomprehensible. Wisdom is nonetheless said to consist in yielding to the obscure forces of a social process that is ordered by a benevolent spontaneity and endowed with a knowledge that is inaccessible to any individual agent. To try to oppose this dynamic in the name of social justice, or to repair the ravages that follow in its wake, would be to turn one's back on the workings of providence in vain pursuit of a will-o'-the-wisp. To the objection that capitalism has manufactured misery by generalizing a form of poverty that was inconceivable in traditional societies, because it combines material want with abandonment to one's own fate— a novel paradox that Marx himself never succeeded in resolving—Hayek's reply is that while capitalism may have multiplied the number of poor, that is because it lets more of them live, that is, survive. Everything takes place, he says, as though evolution performed a "calculus of life," deciding to *sacrifice* some lives so as to make a larger population viable. In any event, if we take an individual at random and ask in what society their chances of leading a full and happy life are maximized, Hayek would surely say that it is in the one that gives free rein to the "spontaneous order" of the market.

Strictly speaking, Hayek's moral philosophy is no more utilitarian or consequentialist than Adam Smith's was. Neither theory makes approval of a particular action contingent on its contribution to "general utility," the reproduction of society, or any other such thing. And yet if human beings are not utilitarians in these masterpieces of economic thought, some other force—God, Nature, Evolution—is called upon to behave in a maximizing fashion on their behalf. Reason does not enlighten them directly; it acts indirectly, by ruse. Indeed, it was economic thought that inspired Hegel's famous cunning of reason. As we saw earlier, this figure, the matrix of modern individualism, is the offspring of Leibniz's monadology, which in turn is inseparable from his theodicy: evil exists because, without it, the sum of good in the world would not be maximized, and ours would not be the best of all possible worlds.

The picture that modernity entertains of itself—inspired by economic thought through and through—is in many ways a consistent one. Nevertheless we must ask whether this consistency is wholly satisfactory from an ethical point of view. Clearly the answer is no. Few elected officials today would be prepared to invoke a higher entity that could justify leaving the weakest individuals by the wayside or regarding the outcasts of industrial society as sacrificial victims whose neglect is a necessary evil. So long as evil was thought to serve good, it thereby seemed justified. Once evil finds itself stripped of meaning, it becomes unbearable. Now that the sacrificial logic has lost its redeeming power, the evils that accompany modern economic growth have progressively lost their rationale. This, I believe, explains why feelings of insecurity have become deeper and more widespread in spite of the fact, or so we are told, that we have never been so safe.

That is essentially a moral explication. Nevertheless there is also a structural dimension to consider. As a statistical matter, life in modern industrial societies may very well be safer than before. But this is chiefly because we have become adept at postponing the most frightening dangers indefinitely. Threats that are ever more horrifying are relegated to a future that itself is pushed back to an ever more distant horizon. To the extent that we imagine ourselves to be in a safe place, it is because we do not see that we are sheltering in the shadow of a far-off apocalypse. During the Cold War, the policy of deterrence used the threat of nuclear apocalypse to prevent its occurrence— such is the paradox inside which that frailest of birds, nuclear peace, made its nest. Other, no less fearsome threats have since appeared on the horizon. Our present, quite relative sense of security is a consequence of sheer luck. In short, we are living on borrowed time. There is no guarantee we will enjoy the same good fortune forever.

CHAPTER 3

Fate, Risk, and Responsibility

> The individual is just foam on the wave, greatness mere
> chance, the perfection of genius but playing with dolls. . . .
> What is it in us that murders, lies, and steals?
> —Georg Büchner, letter to his fiancée, Giessen, 1834

The evil that swoops down on human beings, like a bird of prey, has always had its source in nature and in man's persecution of his fellow man. Pestilence, famine, and war were causes of violent death, which, it was hoped, the development of productive forces and the progress of human wisdom would one day bring to an end. The impotence of human beings to control the sources of evil inspired the idea that destiny, or the will of a god, were responsible for the misfortunes that struck them. The calamities that befall industrial societies today give many people the sense that the tragic fate dreaded by the ancients has returned. The term "risk," applied to climate change, industrial accidents, or public health crises, seems misplaced, for one may well ask who *took* the risk. Because the free thinkers among us seem to have reverted to a religious or mystical interpretation of the world, they are reproached for falling into archaism. Besides, they are told, it is because nobody any longer believes in fate, because responsibility is believed to reside instead with human beings, that the "new" risks of our time are considered to be unacceptable.

I argue in this book on behalf of a "fatalistic" interpretation of the ills that assail us. The fatalism in question is not a response to a lack of power to shape our environment, but rather to an excess of such power, or, more precisely, to our powerlessness to master our own power. As Hans Jonas memorably remarked, "It is no longer nature, as before, but rather our power over it that makes us anxious—both for nature and for ourselves."[1] In order to appreciate the scale of the change, let us return to the picture of the sources of evil that I sketched above.

Nature and persecution are not the only traditional sources of evil. A third one has always been present in people's minds, and if we seek to discover the origin and role of the sacred, it is probably in this direction that we must turn. Here is what Illich said about it in the conclusion of *Medical Nemesis*:

> Man is an animal that can endure trials with patience and learn from them. He is the sole being who knows his own limits and accepts them. He is able to take his own wellbeing in hand because he reacts consciously to pain, to impairment of health and, ultimately, to death. The capacity for revolt and perseverance, for endurance and resignation, are all integral parts of human health.
>
> But even while Man must protect himself on two fronts, against nature and against his neighbor, there exists a third front where the very humanity of Man threatens him. Man must survive his own unhealthy dream, the one that myths molded and kept within limits in all previous cultures. Man has only ever been able to fulfill himself in a society where myths hemmed in the nightmares. It has always been the function of myth to reassure Man on this third front provided that he not overstep the sacred boundaries. The danger of succumbing to this giddiness existed only for those few who tried to outwit the gods. Ordinary mortals died from infirmity or violence. Only he who transgressed the human condition became the prey of Nemesis for having given umbrage to the gods.[2]

"Today," Illich observed, "the physical, social, and psychological consequences of supposedly peaceful enterprises are just as destructive as war."[3]

The main threats that weigh upon the future of the world arise on this third front:

> With the industrialization of desire, Hubris has gone collective and society is the material realisation of the nightmare. The industrial Hubris has shattered the mythic framework that set limits to the folly of dreams. . . . The inevitable aftershock of industrial progress is Nemesis for the masses, that material monster born of the industrial dream. Anonymous, beyond the grasp of computer language, Nemesis has extended its dominion to universal schooling, agriculture, mass transit, industrial wage labor and the medicalization of health. It hovers over television networks, freeways, supermarkets and hospitals. The safety barriers erected by traditional myths have collapsed.[4]

On this view, then, the vengeance wrought by industrial Nemesis manifests itself in the counterproductivity of the major institutions of modern society. Many of the so-called new risks that arouse fear and anxiety today—climate change, environmental catastrophes, unhealthy processed food, contaminated blood transfusions, and so on—are essentially a result of the radical monopoly that a heteronomous mode of production exerts over our relationship not only to our body, to suffering, and to death, but also to our experience of space and time. But they constitute only the tip of the iceberg. That food makes people sick; that medicine kills hospitalized patients with illnesses that doctors themselves acknowledge to be "iatrogenic"; that motorized transport kills people on a grand scale while at the same time destroying nature and polluting the air, exhausting the earth's non-renewable resources, tearing apart cities, devouring leisure time, and creating new forms of dependence—all these dysfunctions are obvious: we see them, hear them, breathe them, and suffer from them every day. And yet it seems no less obvious to most people that those problems can be overcome by means of more and more of the same things that cause them in the first place. This visible part of the counterproductivity iceberg constitutes its technological dimension. But there is an invisible part as well, a hidden evil, that requires us to distinguish between social counterproductivity and structural (or symbolic) counterproductivity. We'll analyze these two dimensions in two major cases: health care and transportation.

Let us begin with health. The great biologist René Dubos proposed that good health be defined as people's autonomous ability to have control over the conditions under which they live, to adapt to accidental modifications of these conditions, and, if need be, to fight against intolerable environments.[5] I do not know a better illustration of the social counterproductivity of medicine than the following lines, taken from a pamphlet distributed in the pharmaceutical industry several decades ago, that explain why France continues to set the world record for the consumption of psychotropic drugs:

> Our age is anxiogenic in a different way [from the "good old days"]: it requires that each person take part in a ceaseless competition in which no one is assured of preserving an acquired advantage. 'Stress' is no less intense than in the past, but now it comes from the increasingly exacting constraints that society imposes on its individual members. Each individual will have to be ever more clear-sighted, alert, and mentally balanced, with rapid and precise reflexes. Nature has endowed few persons with these qualities. The others can rely on a steady supply of tranquilizers in order to maintain themselves at the psychophysiological level necessary for the satisfaction of their ambitions.

And further on, lest it be said that medicine is unconcerned with the economic costs of health, there is this:

> The growing complexity of economic life, currency depreciation, trouble finding employment, the concentration of population in cities, and many other factors of modern life disturb the psychosomatic equilibrium of the individual and often cause pathological states whose treatment, covered by public health insurance, is putting a strain on the national budget. Tranquilizers and sedative-hypnotic drugs serve as preventive and regulative medications that often avoid these complications and are thus a relatively low-cost way to help persons go on working who would otherwise temporarily or permanently withdraw from the economic process.[6]

Doctors' offices are filled with people who have gone on strike. I do not have in mind only labor strikers. There are many other kinds of strike that the law does not contemplate. People may go on strike from their roles as son or daughter, father or mother, spouse or lover, student or teacher, or even corporate executive. All these things are authorized by illness as a social fact. It is accepted that every form of unease or discomfort, whatever its origin or nature—falling behind in school, failure to get along with one's co-workers, unhappiness in one's marriage—can be a reason to seek medical help. Typically the request for assistance disguises the problem as a physical disorder of some sort, with the active complicity of the doctor. The patient need not be a malingerer, nor the physician a fraud. Each is simply playing a game whose rules derive from the social and cultural context of their relationship. Illness is a form of deviance that is tolerated so long as it appears as an organic ailment detachable from its individual or social causes and amenable to a technical treatment. In this way illness acquires an autonomous existence. It is regarded as something external to individuals and their relationship to their environment that happens to disturb their vital functions. This conception of sickness serves as the basis for the tacit agreement between physician and patient, and makes their relationship possible.

The overreliance on institutionalized medicine has an effect, if not also a function: more and more people are convinced that if they feel bad, it is because there is something wrong inside them, and not that their minds and bodies are reacting *in a healthy way* by refusing to adapt to difficult, in some cases unbearable, living conditions. Physicians have even been known to prescribe medications purportedly capable of treating "housing project syndrome" or "workplace anxiety." This medicalization of malaise is both the manifestation and the cause of a loss of personal autonomy: people no longer need nor desire to resolve their problems within the framework of their relations with others. Their capacity for refusing the intolerable withers away, facilitating their withdrawal from the social and political struggle. Thus medicine becomes the alibi of a pathogenic society.

Health, like every use value, can avoid crippling deformation only if what earlier I called the heteronomous mode of production serves to enrich and invigorate the autonomy of both individuals and groups. The heteronomous mode in this case is institutionalized medicine, defined as the set of standardized therapies and treatments dispensed to patients by a corps of specialized professionals. The autonomous mode is what used to be called hygiene. It is significant that this word has lost the value and meaning it once had in relation to the art of living—and of dying. A healthful regimen begins to be stymied when individual producers lose control over their working time and their living conditions. No medico-pharmaceutical crutch can compensate for this kind of alienation. By biologizing and naturalizing the dysfunctions that result from it, medical imperialism prevents intolerable living conditions from being resisted where they should be: in the political arena.

Illich's analysis of the counterproductivity of medicine did not stop at this social critique, however. Self-styled progressives parted ways with him when he went on to suggest that the early treatment of incurable illnesses has the sole effect of aggravating the condition of patients who, in the absence of any diagnosis and any treatment, would remain in good health for the time that is left to them.[7] The philosopher André Gorz was one of the few to take Illich's side. "It has become shocking to state," Gorz observed, "that *it is natural to die*, that there are and *always will be fatal diseases*, that they are not an accidental and avoidable irregularity, but the *contingent form taken by the necessity of death*."[8] Hans Jonas, for his part, likewise noted a fundamental change in this respect: "Death no longer appears as a necessity belonging to the nature of life, but as an avoidable, at least in principle tractable and long-delayable, organic malfunction. . . . These questions involve the very meaning of our finitude, the attitude toward death, and the general biological significance of the balance of death and procreation."[9]

Here we find ourselves on the uncertain boundary that separates the natural from the political. It is this same boundary that distinguishes the structural or symbolic dimension of medical counterproductivity from its social dimension. We must be clear about how these dimensions fit together because they seem to pull in opposite directions. All that today's societies seem capable of doing in the face of so-called new risks is to call for the adoption of "precautionary" policies. Experts disagree whether precaution in this case amounts to action or abstention. The futility of such debates will appear later. Awareness of social counterproductivity orients one toward action, in the political sense of the term, and not primarily toward technology, which serves only as an alibi. Awareness of the symbolic dimension of counterproductivity, by contrast, is identical with the rediscovery of a sense of limits. Is this a matter of action or inaction? The question is idle, and scarcely deserves to be posed.

Structural or symbolic health is the ability to confront with full awareness, and in an autonomous way, not the dangers of the world around us this time, but a series of more intimate threats that every one of us will come to know, namely pain, sickness, and death. People in traditional societies found the ability to face these threats in their culture, which enabled them to give meaning to their mortal condition. The sacred played a fundamental role in this. But the modern world was born on the rubble of traditional symbolic systems and saw in them only the irrational and the arbitrary. In its urge to demystify these systems, modernity failed to understand that by setting limits to the human condition they endowed it with meaning; in replacing the sacred by reason and science, modernity lost all sense of limits and ended up sacrificing meaning itself. The expansion of medicine goes hand in hand with the belief that the complete suppression of pain and disability and the indefinite postponement of death are desirable objectives that can be attained through the unlimited development of the medical system. But one cannot give meaning to what one seeks only to extirpate. Once certain critical thresholds have been crossed, medicine and its myths inexorably destroy the structural conditions of health.

Marx famously identified two sources of alienation. The first lay in the insufficient development of productive forces: incapable of meeting the challenges of their physical environment, vulnerable to poverty and sickness, human beings seek refuge in religious superstition. A second source of alienation is man's exploitation by his fellow man. Here again the exploited confuse the sufferings inflicted by a human oppressor with the will of a god and, numbed by the opium of religion, fail to rise up in revolt. For Marxism, the liberation of humanity entailed struggle on two fronts, against both nature and human oppression. Our analysis of structural or symbolic counterproductivity leads us to ask: beyond which thresholds does the struggle for liberation degenerate into a puerile and absurd rejection of the inevitable? Under what conditions does the mystification that regards evils that arise from political circumstance as facts of nature come to be transformed into an opposite kind of mystification, so that the natural and ineliminable finiteness of the human condition is now perceived as a form of alienation rather than a source of meaning?

I shall say nothing more here about the social counterproductivity of transportation, beyond what I have already said in describing the calculation of the generalized speed of automobiles. The damaging and distorting effects of motorized transport are masked by substituting time spent working for time spent getting from one place to another. By thus making the harm it causes invisible, by advertising itself as a remedy when in fact it is the poison, transportation provides society with an alibi for laying waste to the space and time in which we live our lives. This much is clear. Let us turn, then, to the structural or symbolic dimension of counterproductivity.

Transportation is supposed to give us access to the world and its inhabitants. At the most, transportation may be said to produce conditions favoring the ability of autonomous individuals to enjoy such access. But it can also destroy this very same ability. That is what is happening now.

Autonomy in relation to space is inseparable from low-speed transit that relies for the most part on the metabolic energy of individuals who are the source of their own movement. When we are free of constraints, we choose to walk in pleasurable surroundings. High-speed transit only makes sense when we need to get away from undesirable places or to overcome distances perceived as obstacles. The addiction of industrial societies to high-speed transit shows that their citizens feel at home nowhere, or almost nowhere. If it is true that man "dwells poetically,"[10] the misfortune of living in an uninhabitable place can never be compensated by increasing the opportunities to flee from it as often as possible. People will, Illich wrote, "break the chains of overpowering transportation when they come to love the landscape of their own neighborhood and to dread getting too far away from it."[11] The radical alternative to the current system of motorized transport is not to design quieter and faster means of travel that are less polluting and produce fewer greenhouse gases, but to drastically reduce transportation's hold over our daily life. To do this it is necessary to break the vicious circle by which an industry helps to reinforce the conditions that make it necessary, by which a system of transportation creates the very distances that force people to resort to it.

Space, as human beings have traditionally experienced it, is what topologists call path-connected: any two points can always be connected by a continuous path that remains within the boundaries of the space. Industrial society has shattered this connectedness. Personal spaces are broken up into disjointed pieces, each removed from the other: home, workplace, shops, a few public spaces, and the mythical "elsewhere" of vacation destinations that promise an escape from the crushing tedium of living where one lives. Between these few familiar places lie esthetic and symbolic deserts, soulless wastelands, which one hopes to traverse as efficiently as possible by embracing the system of motorized transport. Thus the spaces crisscrossed by highways through which one travels ensconced in a metal capsule that sometimes turns into a coffin—or the even vaster spaces plied by jet planes.

If the use of motorized transport constitutes a modern ritual, the accompanying myth tells us it will take us home to a traditional neighborhood that no longer exists. The "global village" can be achieved only by *neutralizing* all those meaningless expanses, all those dead spaces waiting to be overcome. The language of advertising, the liturgy of our age, perfectly illustrates the hopes and dreams that the Transportation god is implored to fulfill. One thinks of the advertisement that a Swiss airline once placed in a number of European magazines. It pictures a venerable city, rich in culture and historic architecture, filled with a variety of imposing monuments and squares set along elegant boulevards and sparkling rivers. Looking more closely, however, one realizes that it is a monstrous hybrid juxtaposing the most picturesque districts of Europe's most beautiful cities: a mere riverbed separates Moscow's Red Square from the Place de la Concorde, while Rome's Via Veneto leads directly to Piccadilly Circus. Thanks to our company, the caption proclaims, Europe is reduced to the comfortable dimensions of a single city.

The myths of traditional societies owe their stability to their capacity to conceal the gap between reality and what they say about it—a discrepancy that, once it is perceived, produces what anthropologists call cognitive dissonance. To understand our industrial society's willingness to accept the intolerable absurdity of alienating transportation systems, one must appreciate how thoroughly the myth of return to a primal neighborhood succeeds in masking the obvious, namely, that dead zones take up a great part of the total available time and space: by our calculations, a third of waking existence and as much as half of a city's footprint. The degree to which different modes of locomotion lessen cognitive dissonance varies enormously. At one extreme, walking and bicycling make it possible to enjoy the symbolic richness of the surrounding landscape, but only if this beauty actually exists. At the other extreme, the personal automobile is ideally adapted, much more so than public transportation, to the purpose of supplying society with an alibi for destroying its space and its time. An unsurpassed embodiment of mendacity and blindness, the automobile manages to convey an image of itself that in every respect is contrary to reality: the image conjures up mobility and independence; the reality is a world of traffic jams where each driver is at the mercy of other drivers. It is telling that people describe their car as a bubble that isolates them from a hostile environment, or as an extension of their home—not to say that a sort of umbilical cord that connects them to the places they would like to be, which are never the places they actually are.

The vicious circle of counterproductivity closes on itself as follows. To live in the space-time of industrial society, it is necessary to have access to its system of transportation, which acts as a kind of prosthesis. The existence of this prosthesis removes the incentive to oppose the free play of the forces that shape our space and time. I hardly need to describe these forces, for whether they have to do with land valuation, real estate speculation, or other determinants of the scale and location of economic and social activity, there is no lack of informed analysis, even if interpretations diverge. What is less commonly recognized, however, is the way high-speed transport accelerates the processes of fragmentation and totalization of space. Here Gorz's impassioned plea is more pertinent than ever:

> Never make transportation an issue by itself. Always connect it to the problem of the city, and to the way this compartmentalizes the many divisions of life. . . . The way our space is arranged carries on the disintegration of [personal experience] that begins with the division of labor in the factory. It cuts a person into slices, it cuts our time, our life, into separate slices so that in each one you are a passive consumer at the mercy of the merchants, so that it never occurs to you that work, culture, communication, pleasure, satisfaction of needs, and personal life can and should be one and the same thing: a unified life, sustained by the social fabric of the community.[12]

The problem of identifying the dangers that face us must proceed from an analysis of social and structural counterproductivity. Politicians and philosophers alike often speak as if we found ourselves trapped on an out-of-control train that threatens to crash at any moment into who knows what obstacle. Corinne Lepage describes an "existential vertigo," a "sense of participating in a headlong rush forward that can neither be governed nor stopped. . . . A runaway technological machine, guided solely by a mad urge to press on ever further in a search for every greater profit, has been set in motion."[13] Hans Jonas expresses a similar sentiment: "It is undeniable that we have progressively become the prisoners of processes that we ourselves

Fate, Risk, and Responsibility   35

have unleashed ... without an end having been decided, *almost* as if we were in the grip of fate."[14]

Pascal's vocabulary will be useful here. The "unclever" believe we are in the hands of a fate or destiny that knows where it is going and crushes the human beings it finds in its path. Those who imagine themselves to be clever reject what they see as an archaic and mystical view of the world and try instead to determine who is responsible—which is to say, guilty. Having failed to take the measure of this new economy of evil, the "clever" hope to regulate and contain its dynamic through legal proceedings. That leaves Pascal's "half-clever": the risk managers, insurance economists, and other experts who believe they are in familiar territory because they have learned to discern patterns of probabilizable chance behind the semblance of fate.

None of these approaches seems satisfactory to me. How should we qualify the threats that gather like dark clouds on the horizon, augurs of a disquieting future that seems to be closing in on us? They are neither risks nor a manifestation of fate. If we treat them as risks, conventional distinctions blur. Are they endogenous or exogenous risks? Endogenous, without a doubt, since their source is to be found in human actions, yet simultaneously exogenous, for they appear to threaten us from without. The prototype of exogenous risk used to be the weather. We know now, however, that even the risk of climate change has human causes.

I am going to propose a fourth approach, a paradoxical one that in a sense harks back to the outlook of the "unclever." We must act *as if* we were confronted with fate, precisely in order to deflect it from its otherwise inevitable course. Doom is our destiny, but it is a destiny only because human beings do not recognize in it the consequences of their acts. Above all, it is a destiny that we can *choose* to avert.

CHAPTER 4

The Autonomy of Technology

Everyone fears time, but time fears the pyramids.

—Egyptian proverb

Illich's friend Heinz von Foerster had an entirely different way of looking at counterproductivity. Von Foerster expressed his approach in the form of a conjecture that subsequently, in collaboration with the biophysicist Henri Atlan and the Israeli mathematician Moshe Koppel, I was able to state as a theorem.[1] Our aim was to rigorously describe the relation of circular causality that obtains between a totality or set (a human collectivity, for example) and the elements of this set (the individuals who make up the collectivity). Individuals are linked both to one another and to the set as a whole. The bonds between individuals can be more or less "rigid": the more rigid they are, then by definition, the less information knowledge of one individual's behavior will convey to an observer who already knows how the others behave.

Von Foerster's conjecture says that the more rigid the relations between individuals are, the more the behavior of the totality will appear to its members to be endowed with a dynamic of its own that eludes all efforts on their part to master it. Upon reflection, this is a quite paradoxical thesis. It is valid only so long as one takes the point of view, internal to the system, of the elements

37

interacting within it. For an observer who stands outside the system, by contrast, it goes without saying that rigidity in the relations among the elements favors the attempt to master the system conceptually, for example by means of mathematical modeling. When individuals are rigidly coupled (as a result, say, of mimetic behaviors), von Foerster's conjecture therefore drives a wedge between the internal and external vantage points. The future of the system is predictable, but the individuals inside it feel powerless to affect its course, even though the behavior of the system as a whole is only the aggregate expression of individual reactions to the prediction of this same behavior. The whole seems to break free of the conditions from which it emerged, its trajectory hardening into something that looks very much like fate.

The words I have used to describe the internal view of the totality— "feel," "seems," "appear"—may give the impression that this point of view corresponds to the perceptions of individual subjectivities, which have only to be educated or "wised up" in order to make their perspective coincide with the only objective point of view, the one that the totality of the system has on itself. The implication of von Foerster's theorem, however, is that the internal point of view is every bit as objective as the external point of view. Both are situated points of view, and, in this sense, no more able to be transcended than the situation to which they correspond.

Many are the critics of modern society who have argued that scientific and technological development constitutes an autonomous process that eludes human mastery. Thus, Hans Jonas writes, "Experience has taught us that developments set in motion by technological acts with short-term aims tend to make themselves independent, that is, to gather their own compulsive dynamics, an autonomous momentum, by which they become not only . . . irreversible but also forward-pushing and thus overtake the wishes and plans of the initiators."[2] Heidegger went further than anyone else in this direction, of course, evicting technological thought from its usual habitat, instrumentality. No, technology is not a means in the service of an end, he held; it is destiny (*Geschick*): technology, not humanity, is endowed with autonomy.[3] In France, the philosopher and sociologist Jacques Ellul advanced similar arguments, though on entirely different grounds. A commentator, Dominique Bourg, sums up Ellul's position: "Technology destroys any possibility of making a choice. . . . If one is looking solely for the most efficient means of achieving a given result, there exists by definition only one solution, discover-

The Autonomy of Technology

able by impersonal procedures. The real decision maker is therefore technology itself, in the sense that the decision flows from the logic that presides over the very disposition of means." What is more, Bourg adds, "By its very nature, a technological system has no intentionality. It pursues no particular aim, not even its own growth, which comes about only as a sort of mechanical effect."[4] And Ellul himself concludes: "There can be no human autonomy in the face of technical autonomy."[5]

To make technological evolution a wholly autonomous agent, as some of these authors do, is to fall into the trap of essentialism—precisely the error that von Foerster's theorem avoids by constructing objectivity from the internal point of view. The autonomy of technology, if it exists, is only autonomy *from* this point of view. But saying that is not incompatible with a search for the *mechanisms* that account for such autonomization; or, in Hayekian terms, that explain the *self-exteriorization* of technological phenomena in relation to the conditions that allow them to emerge.[6]

We may look to economists for the rudiments of such an analysis, so long as we are careful to separate it from the optimistic and optimizing ideology that too often pervades their writings. Economists traditionally marvel at the prodigy of social self-regulation that in their view is the market's distinguishing characteristic. The market automatically finds the path leading to equilibrium, which always represents an efficient allocation of resources. What is it that gives the market its capacity for self-organization? The *negative* feedback mechanisms that automatically come into operation when one or more agents stray from equilibrium behavior. The penalty these agents then incur (in the form of falling incomes, bankruptcy, and so on) obliges them either to leave the market or to obey its rules. Free market economists rely on the necessity of giving free play to such mechanisms in order to turn the charge of conservatism back against advocates of social justice. A state that invokes this ideal, in attempting to offset market sanctions by eroding success and compensating failure, they say, freezes existing wealth and stabilizes income disparities while derailing the economic machine.

Now, in recent decades economic theory has begun looking at the role of *positive* feedbacks in market self-regulation, having belatedly come to recognize the importance of imitation in competitive phenomena, particularly with regard to choices among rival technologies. It is well known that imitation produces positive feedbacks, and that these in turn are major sources of dynamic instability. The vast majority of market theorists have ignored imitation. The reasons for this run deep. What is at stake here is the modern conception of both the individual and the social order. Since the self-sufficient and independent individual of economic theory is assumed to be invulnerable to influence from others, it was unimaginable that the collective behavior of market participants might have anything in common with the behavior of crowds and the contagion of acts and emotions from which it springs. And yet, some of the greatest economists of all time—Adam Smith, John Maynard Keynes, Friedrich von Hayek—have granted a central role to imitation.[7] I shall focus here on Hayek because he grasped better than others the conditions and the properties of the self-exteriorization of collective phenomena. The question that arises is how Hayek was able to reconcile his unshakable faith in the self-regulating capacities of the market and his keen appreciation of the importance of imitation. The perplexity is all the more acute in that it arises not only in connection with the market but also with regard to Hayek's theory of cultural evolution, which includes technological development and likewise associates competition, imitation, and efficiency.

The problem that imitation and, more generally, the existence of positive feedback loops pose for any theory of social self-regulation may be grasped by considering a quite elementary model. Two agents A and B reciprocally imitate each other. In principle the object of their mutual imitation is indeterminate. But suppose that some rumor makes A think that B desires (seeks, wants to buy, trusts in, hopes to bring about) object O. Now A knows what to desire and goes after it, thus drawing B's attention to O. When B in turn shows an interest in O, A is led to believe that his initial assumption was correct. However implausible it may have been beforehand, his view of the matter has turned out to be *self-fulfilling*. This process by which an objectivity or exteriority emerges through the closing on itself of a system in which every agent imitates every other, is reinforced as the number of these agents grows. The most absurd rumors can focus a crowd's unanimous attention on the most unexpected object, each person finding the proof of its value in what he takes to be a confirming look or reaction on the part of his neighbors. The process unfolds in two phases. The first is a game of mirrors, at once specular and speculative, in which each person seeks in the others signs that they possess a coveted knowledge, until, sooner or later, everyone is propelled in the same direction. The second phase is the stabilization of the emergent object as the arbitrary conditions of its genesis are forgotten. The unanimity that presided over its birth is enough to project it, at least for a time, outside the system of agents who, all looking in the direction indicated by it, stop casting sidelong glances at each other.

This phenomenological description of the world of imitation can be precisely stated and tested by mathematical modeling. A very active branch of mathematical economics, devoted to exploring the role of what it calls interpersonal influences in economic activity, lets us see how much this mimetic universe differs from an idealized market. Contrary to what one might have expected, and what many authors have in fact assumed, generalized imitation produces something rather than nothing. It sets off self-reinforcing dynamics that converge on their target so consistently that it is difficult to believe this convergence is not the manifestation of an underlying necessity, in the manner of a mechanical or thermodynamical system that invariably returns to its equilibrium state after having been pushed away from it under the effect of some perturbation. Nevertheless it is clear that the concept of equilibrium, imported by market theorists from rational mechanics, is utterly unsuited to characterizing the "attractors" of mimetic dynamics. Far from expressing an implicit order, these dynamics arise from the amplification of an initial disorder, and the impression they give of a predetermined harmony results from a snowballing unanimity. They are condensates, so to speak, of order and disorder. Although mimetic dynamics seem to be guided by a preexisting aim or end—and that is how their operation is perceived from inside the system—in reality the end emerges from the dynamics themselves. Perfectly arbitrary and indeterminate to begin with, it takes on an air of inevitability as the vise of collective opinion gradually tightens. There is no other way of knowing the outcome of a mimetic dynamic than to let it run its course. It is a random procedure that assumes the appearance of necessity.

Equilibrium in the idealized market of the economists is supposed to reflect an external reality: prices express objective values, or "fundamentals," that synthesize a great variety of information regarding available technologies, resource scarcity, consumer preferences, and so on. The dynamic of mimetic behavior, by contrast, is totally closed upon itself. The attractors that it produces reflect no external reality whatsoever, only a condition of internal consistency: namely, the correspondence between a priori beliefs and a posteriori results. Mimetic attractors are self-fulfilling representations.

Generalized imitation has the power, then, to create worlds that are wholly disconnected from reality; worlds that are at once ordered, stable, and completely illusory. It is this "mythopoietic" quality that makes it so fascinating. If there are hidden truths to be discovered somewhere, one must not count on mimetic dynamics to bring them to light. Nor should such dynamics be relied on if efficiency is valued. Efficiency and the capacity for revealing hidden information are two properties that economists like to ascribe to an idealized market. Yet the gap between this ideal and the mimetic process seems unbridgeable.

The main principles of imitative logic may be grasped by considering a very simple model in which the mimetic connections between agents are given and remain fixed during the course of their interaction, with the probability that a given agent will imitate any other agent assumed to be a constant (which can be zero).[8] As an empirical matter it is plain that this assumption is overly restrictive; a mimetic dynamic has the capacity to modify the structure of its own connections so that the probabilities do not remain constant. In reality, the more an agent is already imitated by others, the greater the chance the same agent will be imitated by one more. The power of attraction enjoyed by a particular opinion grows in proportion to the number of individuals who share it. This means that the effects of mimetic snowballing will be still further accentuated. It might seem that such hypotheses overestimate the irrationality of collective phenomena. Research in recent years has shown that the behaviors described may well be individually rational. In some cases, for example, the personal advantage that an individual gains from joining the crowd grows *objectively* in proportion to the latter's size.

Exactly this assumption is now commonly found in the economic literature concerning technology choice. As a technology comes into wider use, more is learned about it, allowing it to be developed and improved. As its users become more numerous, the range of products is expanded and diversified, and both the costs of production and the risks of mechanical failure diminish. Under these circumstances, competition among rival technologies exhibits features that sharply distinguish it from the "perfect competition" of economic doctrine. The first is the multiplicity of "equilibria"—a term that is still current among historians of technology but that, as we saw earlier, is altogether inappropriate; it would be better to speak instead of *attractors*. The "selection" of one attractor rather than another is not deducible from the

The Autonomy of Technology

formal structure of a given situation; only the actual course of events, with all its unforeseeable contingencies, fluctuations, and chance occurrences (especially those that affect the first steps on a given path) will decide the outcome.

A concept plays a crucial role here, that of path-dependence. It is worlds apart from the thermodynamical principles that market theorists are still fond of invoking when they wish to praise the market's capacity to absorb external shocks. The unfolding of a path-dependent dynamic is by its nature highly unpredictable. There is obviously no reason why a technology selected in this way should be the most efficient one possible. One that has been favored by chance at the outset benefits from a "selective advantage" that will be maintained and amplified as the number of users grows. It may end up dominating the market in spite of the fact that some other technology might have proven to be superior had it been chosen at the start. Technological evolution has a strong propensity to become "locked in" to undesirable paths that with the passage of time are increasingly difficult to redirect. Chance, selection, self-organization, the emergence of order through fluctuations: all these phenomena, commonly encountered in the work of historians of technology today, suggest the outlines of a theory of evolution that bears only a very distant relationship to neo-Darwinism.

Technological evolution may therefore give the impression of pointing in a certain direction—as if it embodied an intention, a design, even a destiny—while nonetheless being the result of purely blind mechanisms. There is obviously no guarantee that it will lead us in the "right" direction, if such an idea has any meaning. Indeed, there is no guarantee that it will not lead us to disaster. "The motion once begun takes the law of action out of our hands, and the accomplished facts, created by the beginning, become cumulatively the law of its continuation," Jonas warned. "This heightens the duty to that vigilance over the beginnings which grants priority to well-grounded possibilities of disaster (different from mere fearful fantasies) over hopes, even if no less well grounded."[9]

I now come back to the question I posed earlier. How can someone like Hayek, who founds his social philosophy on a philosophy of mind that assigns a primary role to imitation, avoid so disheartening a conclusion? Very simply. Imagine a world in which everyone imitates everyone else, with the exception of a single individual who imitates no one. It is easy to show that this individual will become the keystone of the system, in that everyone else will end up imitating him and him alone. Let us make one further assumption: this individual imitates no one because he knows his own information to be accurate. The result is an evolutionary process based on imitation that acts as a very efficient means of discovering and disseminating reliable information. But here we must reckon with a troubling property of imitation: its ambivalence. Efficient though it may be if accurate information is available somewhere and recognized as such, imitation otherwise gives rise to illusory inferences and wasteful behavior. The problem is that it is impossible *from within* the system to know which of these two cases obtains. To escape this undecidability, one would have to resort to an external reference point. When a particular evolutionary path attained "truth" or "efficiency," a signal would have to resound, meaning: look no further, stop imitating. The self-exteriorization produced by generalized imitation has optimizing power only if it unfolds within the framework of a genuine exteriority. In the absence of any true exteriority, self-exteriorization can go miserably astray. With regard to the cultural and technological evolution of humanity, the problem is obviously to determine what status one should give this exteriority or transcendence, and to decide who is authorized to speak in its name. There is no escaping the prophets of happiness—though they are less numerous, perhaps, than the prophets of doom. The foremost such prophet of happiness is, of course, none other than Hayek himself.

The analysis of technological autonomy that I have presented here is neither optimistic nor essentialist. In combination with von Foerster's theorem it will help us to demystify the category of fate, to draw aside what Marx called the "mystical veil" that prevents alienated human beings from seeing the world as it is. *Pure mechanisms can mimic the workings of fate.* The apostles of technology have long embraced this lesson, fascinated as they are by the prospect of creating autonomous artifacts. John von Neumann, inventor of the theory of automata and a pioneer of the electronic computer, predicted in 1948 that the day would come—sooner rather than later, he believed—when the builders of such machines would feel as perplexed before their creations as we ourselves feel before complex natural phenomena.[10] The quasi-theological exhilaration of fabricating an automaton, which is to say a creature that lays down the rules of its own behavior; the overwhelming will to power manifested by the desire to be the cause of a being that is the unconditioned cause of itself; the desire to lose oneself in the mirror held up by a creature made in one's own image—under the awful sway of these irresistible urges, technology is carried off in directions that fill with holy dread even its most zealous apologists.[11] Research on artificial intelligence, robotics, artificial life, genetic algorithms, biocomputing, and nanotechnologies will increasingly blur the boundaries that, in separating the world of the living from that of machines, the world of the mind from that of mechanisms, help us still today to give meaning to the human condition. Everything takes place as though technology, by seizing ever greater autonomy for itself, were destined to incarnate an inhuman fate that would finally relieve humanity of the burden of freedom.

CHAPTER 5

Doomsaying on Trial

[Fear] is not pretty to look at—not at all!—sometimes
mocked, sometimes cursed, disowned by all. . . . And yet,
make no mistake: it always appears at the deathbed, interceding on our behalf.

—Georges Bernanos, *Joy* (1929)

When the age of apparently limitless postwar economic growth abruptly came to an end after only thirty years, in 1975 or so, the radical critique of industrial society and its model of development lost its appeal as well. Even so, young people today should not suppose that Illich's ideas were wholly without influence. Words such as "conviviality" and "counterproductivity" entered the language thanks to his writings, which even left their mark on the very professionals and technocrats who could or should have felt themselves to be the targets of his criticism. To be sure, it was educators who recognized the force of Illich's denunciation of medicine and doctors who saw the value of his attack on transportation! Unemployment had become stubbornly entrenched, however, and growth appeared to be the only way out. It no longer seemed to matter how the growth was achieved. Macroeconomics was in the driver's seat, and people stopped ask-

47

ing fundamental questions. Growth and its proper distribution were now the sole objects of public concern. But however fine a thing it may be to wish to share fairly the largest possible pie, one should perhaps look first to be sure the pie is not poisoned.

In the meantime the harms and dangers associated with the industrial model of development had not disappeared. Eventually the greatest fears of the age came to be summed up in a single phrase, recited like the chant of a propitiatory rite: "the precautionary principle." I should like to make it clear that the present work is not a study of this principle. I do not seek to define it, still less to propose a philosophical foundation for it. Nor do I pretend to substitute another, more satisfactory principle for it. As will be seen, my "enlightened doomsaying" does not aspire to the status of a principle. Enlightened doomsaying is a philosophical attitude, a metaphysical challenge to our usual ways of thinking about the world and about time that is based on the peculiar temporality of catastrophes. Nonetheless, all those who have reflected on the precautionary principle—and they are many, not only economists and legal scholars but sociologists and political scientists as well—have been a great help to me. But they have helped me less by what they contribute than by what they reject. The expression "doomsaying" does not originally have a positive connotation. It is the pejorative way theorists writing about precaution characterize the "absolutist" position they decry.

During the Cold War, the expression "mutually assured destruction" and its acronym MAD were initially used by those who considered the doctrine of nuclear deterrence to be pure insanity. They may not have been wrong. Remarkably, however, the champions of this doctrine hastened to reappropriate the label and managed to make it respectable. I hope to be able to do the same thing for "doomsaying."

The version of "doomsaying" attacked by theorists writing about precaution is an easy target, for it is indeed unrealistic, contradictory—in short, untenable. But it is a crude caricature, even if, here and there, sometimes at the highest levels of government, one can find such unrigorous thinking invoked or defended in the name of the precautionary principle. The demonstration would be more convincing if it proved that *any* doomsaying stance is necessarily vulnerable to similar criticism. My goal is to show how, on the contrary, one may construct a form of doomsaying that is consistent and compatible with the most exacting rationality.

Theorists generally level three criticisms at the precautionary attitude toward risk or uncertain threats: it supposedly aims at "zero risk," contemplates only "worst-case scenarios," and demands that the "burden of proof" be reversed, so that it becomes the responsibility of the manufacturer or inventor to demonstrate the complete safety of a new product, and not of potential victims to prove its harmfulness. But, the critics object, "zero risk" is an impossible and paralyzing ideal. Furthermore, they add, because we live in a world of scientific "controversy," no incontestably worst case can ever be defined; the concept is evanescent. Finally, they say, because ours is inescapably an uncertain world, innocuousness is impossible to prove. The critics conclude that the absolutist conception with which they identify every kind of apocalyptic prophecy cannot fail to lead to a policy of abstention, which is to say of inaction.[1]

Everyone will agree that "zero risk" is an unattainable ideal that would hinder action. But that is not what the argument is about. "Hiding behind the constant refrain 'zero risk does not exist,' which is obvious," observes Corinne Lepage, "is a real refusal to seriously apply the precautionary principle, which alone is capable of rationalizing and humanizing progress."[2] I quite agree—except for the reference to the precautionary principle. In the position that I defend, not only does risk—or, as I will say, catastrophe— remain a possibility, but only the inevitability of its future realization can induce prudence. The notion of a worst-case scenario is admittedly fuzzy. For any action that is undertaken or any policy that is agreed upon, how far can pessimism reasonably be allowed to extend? A nuclear energy plant was built about sixty miles upriver from Paris: did anyone think about the possibility of a Chernobyl-on-the-Seine? Genetically modified plants are cultivated on a large scale: must we focus on a scenario where resistant genes proliferate and fatally contaminate natural habitats? Artificial intelligence and nano-technology research laboratories throughout the world are trying to create intelligent robots endowed with consciousness: did it occur to anyone that one day such machines might reduce us to slavery and even annihilate the human race? But since, by hypothesis, the world is inherently uncertain, why should we believe that the worst is certain to happen?

Here I am afraid the critics are making a logical mistake. The point at issue here is a very subtle one, and I must ask my readers to pay especially close attention, for they will be able to grasp the solution I propose only if this point is perfectly clear. The critics mistakenly assume that doomsaying aims at "zero risk," the complete absence of damage. From this they infer that doomsaying focuses on the worst-case scenario in order to ensure that there will be no damages even in the direst of circumstances. It may be conceded that this way of proceeding would lead to a policy of generalized "abstention." Of course, anyone today who spent their life shut up in their room, as Pascal advised, would still run the risk of perishing in a gas explosion or from an airplane crashing through the roof. However, the critics seem not to see that one may focus on the worst-case scenario, not as something that can or must occur *in the future*, but as something that could or would occur *if* one were to act in a certain way. In the first instance, the worst-case scenario has the character of a *prediction*. In the second, it is a *conditional* hypothesis that helps us to choose, from among a range of options, the one (or ones) that will make the worst case acceptable; or, a variant of this, the option that will reduce as far as possible the damages caused by the worst case. In the theory of decision under uncertainty, this last approach is called "minimax," for it is meant to *mini*mize the *max*imum possible damage. I will come back to this. For the moment it needs to be pointed out that "minimizing the worst"— if I may be forgiven for using such a barbarism—does not mean making it innocuous. This point of logic cannot help calling to mind Leibniz's theodicy, which I mentioned earlier. Why is there evil in the world? Because our world is the best of all possible worlds. This answer has been an object of mockery since the time of Voltaire, but it is nevertheless perfectly coherent. The world that minimizes evil does not thereby reduce it to zero. To confuse the least evil possible with its complete absence is to commit a category error.

However, my approach will be very different. I quite agree with Corinne Lepage when she says, "It is the absurdity of destruction that prompts us to turn to the worst-case scenario. It is the relevance, not to say the simple existence of the possibility of this worst case that can and must inform thought and action."[3] Precisely because catastrophe is an abhorrent fate that no one can wish for, we are obliged to keep our eyes fixed on it and never lose sight of it. I fear this idea will make little sense to those whose job is to manage risk. What they see is that, for *any one* of the risks they are concerned with, it is unlikely that the future holds a major tragedy in store for us. Climate change, the pollution of the oceans, the dangers of nuclear energy or genetic engineering, the outbreak of new epidemics or endemics—whatever comes along, humanity will always adapt or find a technical fix. This is the terrifying thing about a catastrophe: not only does no one *believe* that it will occur, even though there is every reason for *knowing* that it will occur; but once it has occurred it appears to be a part of the normal order of things. Its very reality suddenly makes it seem banal, commonplace. Having not been considered possible before it actually came about, it takes its place without further ado among all the other things that constitute what philosophers call the "ontological furniture" of the world. I quoted in the prologue the words of Bergson on discovering that Germany had declared war on France: "who would have thought that so terrible an eventuality could make its entrance into reality with so little fuss? This impression of simplicity was predominant above all else." Less than two months after the collapse of the World Trade Center, the American authorities had to remind their countrymen of the extreme gravity of the event so that the desire for justice and revenge would not weaken.[4] The twentieth century is proof that the worst abominations can be absorbed by the collective consciousness without any particular difficulty. The serenely calculating rationality displayed by risk managers today flows from the remarkable capacity of human beings to resign themselves to the intolerable. It is the most manifest symptom of that unrealistic attitude that deals with "risks" by taking them out of the general context to which they belong.

This spontaneous metaphysics of the temporality of catastrophes is, as I will try to show, the prime obstacle to defining a form of prudence adapted to our time. But this very same metaphysics, I believe, contains the solution to the problem. Once again, the poison will serve as remedy. With regard to the question of worst-case scenarios, my method will be to reason as if regarding a catastrophe as possible were equivalent to thinking not only that it will occur but that it will *necessarily* occur. This equivalence must not be interpreted as a sort of special license granted to doomsayers, who are thereby allowed to convert the least cause for trepidation into certain disaster. It is to be understood instead as constituting a constraint on what can be taken to be possible.[5] The possible exists only in present and future actuality,[6] and this actuality is itself a necessity. More precisely, before a catastrophe occurs, it is possible for it not to occur; it is in occurring that it begins to have always been necessary, and therefore that non-catastrophe, which until then had been possible, begins to have always been impossible.

Here the paradox of Bergson's metaphysics reappears, but with a crucial modal reversal. It is no more true in the metaphysics I propose than in Bergson's that one can "work backwards in time." But in mine, what spontaneously embeds itself in the past as reality goes on creating itself is not, as in Bergson, the possible, but rather the impossible. Recall that before the war broke out, it appeared to Bergson as "*at once probable and impossible*: a complex and contradictory idea that lasted right down to the fateful day." The metaphysics that I advance as a foundation for a prudence adapted to a time of catastrophes is no less complex, but it can be shown, I believe, to be free of contradiction. It requires us to *project ourselves*, by a leap of the imagination, into the aftermath of the catastrophe, and then to look back on it retrospectively as an event that was *both necessary and improbable*.

These ideas are not easily grasped, and one may wonder whether it is really necessary to resort to formulations of this kind. But I see no alternative. The chief obstacle that keeps us from meeting the threats that weigh on the future of humanity is, I contend, conceptual in nature. We have acquired the means to destroy the planet and ourselves, but we have not changed our ways of thinking. Many people seem to suppose that it is enough to devise new procedures of deliberation and decision, democratic or otherwise. Yet there is little reason to believe that such procedures are capable by themselves of resolving problems that have been a source of vexation and puzzlement for philosophy (and metaphysics in particular) from the earliest times. One senses that the relevant questions have to do with the future, with time and temporality. Catastrophe may be located in the future, but is that future real? Prophets of doom announce that catastrophe is imminent, but is such prediction or prophecy even possible, and what claim can it have to objectivity, insofar as the future has no causal effect on the past? If a true prophecy can be uttered about the future, is that incompatible with the exercise of free will, understood as the capacity to act otherwise than one does? What can one say about possibilities that will not have been actualized? Can one cross the probable and the possible modes by defining probabilities over conditional propositions of the type: "If we had done this—when we actually did that—such-and-such a catastrophe would have been avoided"?

All of these are among the most ancient problems in philosophy—and answers to them must somehow be found if we are to meet the challenges of our age. Those who deem philosophy a gratuitous activity are no less mistaken than those who believe they can do without it. When a government official declares that "in a situation characterized by risk, a hypothesis that has not been invalidated should provisionally be held to be valid, even if it has not been formally demonstrated,"[7] his words are loaded with a great many philosophical assumptions that need to be made explicit. I choose to quote this formula, in particular, because in spite of its imprecision it is not so very far removed from the metaphysical reversal that I am suggesting. Hans Jonas, writing about "unacceptable" risks, expands on the same idea much more rigorously: "We have here an inversion of Descartes's principle of doubt. In order to ascertain the indubitable truth we should, according to Descartes, equate everything doubtful with the demonstrably false. Here on the contrary we are told to treat, for the purposes of decision, the doubtful or possible as if it were certain, when it is of a certain kind. It is also a subspecies of [Pascal's] wager."[8]

The foregoing developments were necessary to refute the idea that worst-case scenarios are a wretched guide for action. We now come to the third objection brought against doomsaying, namely, that it stands the usual burden of proof on its head by unreasonably requiring that every proposed innovation first demonstrate its harmlessness. Such a demonstration is said to be impossible, however, owing to the dissymmetry between confirmation and falsification identified by Karl Popper. For the claim of harmlessness to be disproved, it suffices merely to adduce a single case of harm. But the absence of harm cannot be proven, since this would require submitting to an infinite number of tests a universally quantified proposition of the type: "In every case or context x, product y is not harmful."

This third objection is easily disposed of. It assumes that shifting the burden of proof requires that one demonstrate a *complete* absence of risk. But that is not so. The reference to Popper serves here as a smokescreen, for it prevents us from seeing a clear and uncomplicated idea that underlies probabilistic reasoning in most of the applied sciences: it is not true that the absence of a proof that p (where p, for example, stands for the proposition "Product y is harmful") suffices to demonstrate not-p (in this case, "Product y is not harmful"). In other words, the fact that p has not been proved does not imply that not-p has been proved.

Let us imagine that you have some reason to doubt the integrity of a coin that is to be used in a game of heads or tails, say because it seems unbalanced in a way that favors tails. You toss it three times in a row and each time it does indeed come up tails. If this were the result of chance—which is to say if the coin were in fact properly balanced—the a priori probability of obtaining three tails in a row would be one-half cubed, or one-eighth (12.5%). By convention, it is accepted in statistics that a probability higher than 5% *does not suffice* to reject the hypothesis that a result is due to chance. Why 5%, rather than 45%, for example, or 33%? This threshold is surely to some extent arbitrary, but it well conveys the notion of a *burden* of proof. If one is to prove that the coin is unbalanced, one must do more in the way of research and experiment in order to justify a degree of conviction that is beyond a reasonable doubt. In the present case, because the result is well within the bounds of normal probability, one must admit that it is not proven that the coin is unbalanced. It would be a flagrant sophism, however, to conclude from this that it has been proven not to be unbalanced. It may be the case, after all, that neither a proposition nor its negation is proved.[9] One often encounters the claim that such-and-such a product has been proven to be perfectly harmless, whereas in fact the most that can be said is that no one has succeeded in proving that it is harmful.

That the nature and status of proof in this case should be a subject of dispute reminds us that, until fairly recently, the absence of any showing that a technological or commercial innovation was harmful was generally thought to be enough to justify the conclusion that it was not in fact harmful. If from now on innovators are required to prove that a new product or procedure is safe, should we regard this as an outrageous imposition? Surely the relevant question must be: on whom does the burden of proof fall? The answer depends on the logic of the situation and on the values of the society faced with it. In the case of a criminal trial, for example, between a miscarriage of justice that leads to the sentencing of an innocent person and one that leads to the release of a guilty person, the first error is held to be by far the more serious of the two in Western societies. This is why we require the prosecution to prove, beyond a reasonable doubt, that the defendant is in fact guilty. That the accused may not have succeeded in establishing his innocence cannot offset the state's obligation to establish his guilt.[10]

Similarly, what could be more in keeping with common sense if, in the case of potentially serious or irreversible damages, one were to hold that it is better to err on the side of assuming the likelihood of harm than the oppo-

Doomsaying on Trial

site? It is altogether natural, then, that the burden should fall upon the innovator to prove that an innovation is not harmful, since the absence of proof that it is harmful absolutely does not suffice. Consider the present situation with scientific journal articles on genetic engineering. A recent study shows that they consistently commit the sophism I just mentioned in connection with the tossing of a coin, even though they claim to apply the precautionary principle.[11] Does the reversal of the burden of proof constitute an unreasonable standard? No, for it does not entail conclusively demonstrating a complete absence of harm. It asks us instead to establish innocuousness *beyond a reasonable doubt*; that is, to reduce to less than 5% the a priori probability that experimental results seeming to confirm the assumption of innocuousness are due to chance. The justice of this demand will be recognized by every responsible person. Everyone should be able to agree on the need to devote sufficient research funds to this purpose—and that there is nothing in the least objectionable about reversing the usual burden of proof with regard to the possibility of catastrophic accident.

I have already mentioned several times Hans Jonas's book *The Imperative of Responsibility*, which in its original German edition[12] did much to popularize the idea of precaution (*Vorsorge*) in the countries of northern Europe in the 1980s and 1990s. French theorists of precaution feel obliged to refer to it while hastening to say they have nothing to do with the argument that Jonas develops there. It is nevertheless important to read this difficult book carefully. In general only a few phrases are quoted from it—always the same ones, as though repeating them often enough will dispel the whiff of brimstone.

To believe Jonas's critics, his argument is a distillation of everything that is exaggerated and alarmist about the catastrophist position. He presents himself, deliberately, as a prophet of doom; his thinking is shot through and through with theology; he calls upon us to interpret our predicament, and the grave responsibility it places upon us, under the influence of fear—an attitude that he himself calls the "heuristics of fear." Radicalism of this sort, it is said, can have the effect only of paralyzing action and ultimately requiring it to be ratified and enforced by a totalitarian regime.

Indeed, it is true that in *The Imperative of Responsibility* Jonas urges his readers "to allow, in matters of such capital eventualities, more weight to threat than to promise, and to avoid apocalyptic prospects even at the price of thereby perhaps missing eschatological fulfillments."[13] Put more simply: "The prophecy of doom is to be given greater heed than the prophecy of bliss."[14] This means that "in matters of a certain magnitude—those with apocalyptic potential—greater weight [must be given] to the prognosis of doom than to that of salvation. The premise of the whole argument [is] that both today and in the future we will have to deal with actions of just that magnitude, which is itself a *novum* in human affairs."[15] I believe that the soundness of this position can be demonstrated, not in a mood of fear and trembling, but with all the resources of a cool head and clear mind; and that there are good grounds for believing that the brand of doomsaying espoused by Jonas is wholly rational.

Jonas's critics recoil from his "heuristics of fear." How can one deliberate, or even think, when seized by fear or in the grip of panic? Thus Catherine Larrère: "The 'prophecy of doom' . . . rules out any possibility of choosing. . . . The choice of the worst-case scenario precludes all democratic debate: under the threat of imminent catastrophe, deliberation is not possible."[16] This utterly mistakes Jonas's meaning. His point of departure is the same as mine, namely, that the prospect of catastrophe, so far from moving us to act, leaves us perfectly indifferent. As Bergson perceived on the eve of the First World War, the catastrophe seems to us impossible. It is precisely in order to overcome this obstacle, which is more metaphysical than psychological, that Jonas proposes first and foremost a method. The heuristics of fear is not an excuse for turning away from reason, for letting ourselves be carried away by a floodtide of emotion. It is a way of exploiting a simulated, imagined sense of dread in order to discover which things in life we value above all others.

Jonas's critics seem to have forgotten that the first truly modern philosophy, the matrix of the tradition of mechanistic rationalism, rests precisely on a relation to fear. Breaking utterly with ancient thought, Thomas Hobbes renounced building an ideal polity on a conception of the good accepted by all. He had witnessed at first hand the tragic events of the civil war that tore apart England in the middle of the seventeenth century, and seen that men fight and kill one another in the name of rival conceptions of what is right and true. Civil peace could therefore be founded only on the basis of the one thing that they have in common—not some idea of the good, but a shared apprehension of evil: the fear of violent death. For this reason Hobbes is generally regarded as the father of liberalism, even though the political solution that he recommends amounts to rationalizing the absolute power of the state. The paradox is merely apparent. As Hobbes had shown at the

Doomsaying on Trial

dawn of modern philosophy, rationality and fear are in no way incompatible.

Jonas himself refers to Hobbes while making clear what separates him from his predecessor. It is not ourselves but our children or our children's children who may fall victim to catastrophe if we are not able to prevent it by acting before it is too late. In Hobbes's world, each person gives absolute priority to his own survival. In ours, Jonas says, "that which is to be feared has never yet happened and has perhaps no analogies in past or present experience." Hence the "creatively imagined *malum*" has to take over the role of the directly experienced *malum*. Conjuring up the necessary representation by turning one's thoughts to the future becomes the primary obligation. "But one sees at once," Jonas adds, "that this imagined and distant evil, which is not mine, will not arouse fear as naturally and spontaneously as does a present danger which threatens [me] or those near to me." The situation "is thus not as simple as it was for Hobbes, who also, instead of love for a *summum bonum*, made fear of a *summum malum*, namely, the fear of a violent death, the starting point of morality."[17]

Jonas's critics reproach his thinking for being steeped in theology. This objection derives from a confusion between theology and metaphysics, which are, it is true, two kindred branches of speculative thought. Jonas's real purpose is to construct a secular ethics. Like Illich, he asks "whether, without restoring the category of the sacred, the category most thoroughly destroyed by the scientific enlightenment [*Aufklärung*], we can have an ethics able to cope with the extreme powers which we possess today and constantly increase and are almost compelled to wield." His conclusion is unambiguous: "Religion in eclipse cannot relieve ethics of its task."[18] But theology is held up, like fear, as the enemy of rational thought. I have argued, along with Jonas, that metaphysics is indispensable to our present purpose. Like metaphysics, theology is, or can be made to be, a rational discipline. Yet the spirit of our age tells us otherwise. It says that genuinely ethical reflection can survive only if it is snatched from the jaws of religion: to be moral, one must be an atheist. The blindness of this view has been amply demonstrated elsewhere.[19]

As for the charge that Jonas's absolutism can lead only to *inaction*, he has already disposed of it in advance. The fear that is an essential part of responsibility, he emphasizes, is not one that advises against acting, but that encourages action. After all, no *action* expresses human liberty more strongly than setting limits to the individual capacity for action, in the form of universally valid imperatives, norms, and rules, and then adhering to them. It is through such self-limitation that individuals come to interact with one another as autonomous persons. Does this inevitably entail a descent into political totalitarianism? Plainly the opposite is true. Either democratic debate over new threats to humanity will increasingly be concerned with the limits that industrial societies are willing to impose on themselves, in coordination with one another, or else a terrifying regime of ecofascism may rear its head.

It is nevertheless true that hints of a rather disturbing authoritarian sensibility may sometimes be found in Jonas's writings.[20] However, an exhaustive critical reading is not a task I can undertake here. In what follows I shall leave to one side whole strands of Jonas's work, in particular everything having to do with his ontology of the good, and limit myself to discussing a few salient points that overlap with my own approach. Jonas's writings are filled with dazzling philosophical intuitions whose implications need to be teased out. For the better part of a century now, philosophy has been split in two branches, an "analytic" school, inspired by research in mathematical logic and written chiefly in English, and a "Continental" school, heir to the phenomenological tradition and written chiefly in French and German. Independent minds care little about this schism. Jonas recognized that he was to some extent an outsider to the philosophical life of the twentieth century, having for more than seventy years held himself "apart from the mainstream, and more particularly from the powerful current of analytic philosophy."[21] My own view is that Jonas could have found the intellectual tools he lacked in the rational theology and metaphysics that this very same tendency has done so much to deepen and enrich.[22] I share with Jonas the conviction that our current situation obliges us to give priority not only to ethics over politics but also to metaphysics over ethics. Faith "thus can very well supply the foundation for ethics, but it is not there on command," Jonas notes. "Metaphysics on the other hand has always been a business of reason, and reason can be set to work on demand. . . . The worldly philosopher struggling for an ethics must first of all hypothetically allow the *possibility* of a rational metaphysics, despite Kant's contrary verdict."[23] The "deconstruction" of Western metaphysics began long before Derrida, of course, with Kant himself. Analytic philosophy, to its credit, has never allowed itself to be intimidated by the "deconstructionist" enterprise of either.

Finally, I confess that not the least of the things about Jonas that I find fascinating is his name, which harks back to another prophet of doom from twenty-eight centuries earlier.[24] Mysticism is not in my nature, but I cannot help thinking that in this magnificent coincidence we may catch a glimpse of fate winking its eye at us. Jonas is a great annoyance to theorists of precaution, who would like nothing better than to throw him overboard, as foreign sailors did in the case of his namesake, Jonah. I shall show that the misadventures of this distant ancestor, the paragon of all scapegoats, go straight to the heart of the metaphysical reversal that I am proposing.

PART TWO

The Limits of Economic Rationality

CHAPTER 6

Precaution, Between Risk and Uncertainty

Wisdom does not consist in taking all manner of precautions indiscriminately, but in choosing those that are useful and neglecting those that are superfluous.

—Jean-Jacques Rousseau, *Julie, or the New Heloise* (1761)

There is no avoiding the precautionary principle. But if it has a place in the law of both France and the European Community, the definitions and accompanying commentaries that one finds there sometimes give the comical impression of attempting to describe with great precision an object whose very existence is uncertain. Since the whole point of the precautionary principle is to legislate with regard to risks whose very existence is uncertain, perhaps the idea of applying the principle to itself ought to be taken seriously.[1] I shall return to this idea in due course.

Prudence (or practical wisdom, which Aristotle called *phronesis*) was traditionally concerned with the choice of means suitable to ends. The modern theory of prudence (or is it the theory of modern prudence?) is for the most part identical with the theory of rational choice developed by John von Neumann and Leonard Savage during and after the Second World War. It provides the framework within which risk managers everywhere now think,

63

calculate, and reason about the future, whether they are working on the safety of a program of major scientific and commercial importance, such as the NASA manned spaceflight program, or designing new forms of insurance made necessary by recent advances in genetic engineering. The age-old notion of risk prevention fits perfectly into this framework. Sometimes an ounce of prevention is worth a pound of cure: the "cost-benefit" approach (which is only another name for rational choice theory) tells us when that is the case. One compares the costs of a preventive action, which in general are rather well known, with its anticipated benefits, which in the case of a random event are known only probabilistically. Sometimes the uncertainty is such that it cannot be characterized with reference to calculable probabilities, at least insofar as such probabilities are supposed to reflect an observable frequency. In that case many other techniques of estimation can be employed, among them the minimax method, which, as we saw in the previous chapter, involves minimizing the maximum prospective harm, and the Bayesian treatment of subjective probabilities, to which I shall turn in a moment.

Let us begin by addressing the most intriguing question raised by debate over the precautionary principle. What made anyone suppose that the existing philosophy of decision under uncertainty was inadequate to deal with new "risks" associated with the environment, health, food production, or industrial activity? Why did anyone feel the need to supplement the notion of prevention with that of "precaution"? It would be too facile to reply that the scale of the new threats, and the degree of uncertainty surrounding them, requires a new approach. As the modern form of prudence, rational choice theory was intended to have universal validity. Unsurprisingly, perhaps, the economists who have latched onto the new concept subject it to the same tried-and-true methods they have always used. Kourilsky and Viney, in the report on the precautionary principle delivered to the French prime minister in January 2000, take note of this situation, and suggest that the "mutual convergence of precaution, prevention, and prudence might justify replacing the precautionary principle by a prudential principle that would encompass precaution and prevention." Indeed, they come close to taking this step themselves, for they go on at once to say that, within a framework of prudence, "the precautionary principle recognizes the social obligation to reinforce prevention and to apply preventive methods in novel ways."[2]

It will be obvious that the theory of precaution in its present form suffers from vagueness, contradiction, and inconsistency. It is not my ambition, as I said, to try to save the theory. I observe only that its defects are a consequence of the awkward predicament in which the theory's defenders find themselves. On the one hand, they seek to identify something unprecedented about the new threats that would warrant approving an approach that is itself unprecedented. On the other hand, anxious to conform to accepted ideas of reasonableness and rationality, they unfailingly fall back on the same models and methods that they have always relied on. Let me be blunt: the doctrine of precaution remains hostage to the cost-benefit orientation of rational choice theory.

Consider, for example, the version of the precautionary principle found in the first article of the French law of February 2, 1995, mandating stronger environmental protection (the so-called Barnier law): "An absence of certainty, due allowance having been made for the current state of scientific and technological knowledge, must not delay the adoption of effective, proportionate measures aimed at preventing a risk of grave and irreversible damage to the environment at an economically acceptable cost."[3] In this formulation one detects an uneasy tension between the logic of economic calculation and a dawning awareness that the context of decision-making has radically changed; between, on the one hand, the familiar and reassuring notions of efficiency, commensurability, and reasonable cost, and, on the other, the lack of sure knowledge and the prospect of grave and irreversible harm. It would be all too easy to point out that, given the fact of uncertainty, no one can say what measure is proportionate to a damage whose order of magnitude is unknown, and of which one therefore cannot say whether it will be serious or irreversible; nor can anyone evaluate what the cost of adequate prevention would be, or say how, in the event that this cost should turn out to be "unacceptable," society ought to choose between saving the economy and preventing catastrophe.

The plain fact of the matter is that theoretical economists and insurance experts have invested too much time and effort in wheeling out their wonderful calculating machines to let them stand idle. Nevertheless it will be worth our while to travel a bit farther in their company, for the theory of decision under uncertainty, on which their approach to these questions rests, has considerable analytical resources. We owe it to ourselves to examine them more closely before coming to any firm judgment as to their inadequacy.

Uncertainty and Subjective Probabilities

The notion of risk takes on its full meaning in the context of games of chance, which, as we saw earlier, first inspired probability theory and research on optimal betting strategies. Suppose that I am charged an entrance fee of $60 in order to play a coin-tossing game in which I stand to win $200 if the coin turns up heads and to lose $100 if it turns up tails. In that case it is rational to decide not to play. This can easily be shown by multiplying the gains and losses by their respective probabilities, which have an objective basis in the relative frequencies with which the corresponding events occur. It was tempting to extend this approach, by analogy, to all sorts of decisions that can be thought of as wagers. I make a bet, it might be said, when I risk money in the stock market, an institution that is often likened to a gigantic casino. One might also say that I make a bet in investing in this or that sector of the economy, though commercial activity may seem less obviously to resemble a game of chance. I make a bet in deciding to go hiking in the mountains or in boarding a plane to cross the ocean. I make a bet in choosing to marry. If Pascal was right, I even make a bet in deciding whether or not to believe in God.

It was not until 1921 that two eminent economists, Frank Knight and John Maynard Keynes, protested that this way of looking at things is inappropriate where it is impossible, or at least very difficult, to assign objective probabilities to events, either because they occur only once or because their frequencies are unobservable. In books published separately the same year, Keynes[4] and Knight[5] introduced a fundamental distinction between two types of uncertainty: risk and irreducible or intrinsic uncertainty. Risk obtains when the uncertainty is probabilizable, because relative frequencies can be observed and compared. In the contrary case, when no measurement is possible, one is said to be in the presence of irreducible uncertainty (or simply uncertainty, as I shall call it from now on). The question naturally arises whether rules of action can be formulated to cope with uncertainty, by analogy with the laws that govern wagers in the case of risk. Both Keynes and Knight had very interesting things to say on this point, but their suggestions were for the most part to remain without effect, for reasons that will soon become clear.

Even if the Kourilsky-Viney report is not as precise or clear as one might have hoped, it distinguishes between two kinds of risk—one "potential," the

Precaution, Between Risk and Uncertainty 67

other "proven"—in a way that seems partly to coincide with our distinction between uncertainty and risk: "The distinction between potential risk and proven risk forms the basis for a parallel distinction between precaution and prevention. Precaution is associated with potential risks and prevention with proven risks."[6] Potential risk, the report goes on to say, is not a risk waiting to be realized (in which case, it should be noted in passing, the word "potential" is poorly chosen); it is a "risk of risk," something that is no more than a conjectural risk. It would be clearer to say that potential risk corresponds to a dangerous event that may or may not occur (as in the case of every event subject to hazard or chance), where the likelihood of its occurring cannot precisely be estimated. Since we are told that precaution stands in the same relation to potential risks as prevention to proven risks, one is tempted to conclude that the first configuration corresponds to the case of what we are calling uncertainty.

But the Kourilsky-Viney report does not stop there. Having introduced the notion of a risk of risk, it tries to smuggle in behind it the notion of a probability of probability. The fact that no probability can be assigned to an uncertain event is taken to mean that there is indeed a probability, only it is unknown. Nevertheless this unknown probability can itself be assigned a probability, or rather a distribution of probabilities. "The probabilities are not of the same kind: in the case of precaution," the report emphasizes, "one is dealing with the probability that a particular hypothesis is accurate; in the case of prevention, the degree of danger is established and one is dealing with the probability that an accident will occur."[7] Thus one might state, for example, that a probability e is attributed to the *hypothesis* that a nuclear power plant C has a probability $1 - n$ of experiencing a critical accident over the next twenty years, n being the probability that it will operate safely, without any major accident; and that a probability $1 - e$ is attributed to the *hypothesis* that it is certain the same nuclear power plant will experience no accident.

Ultimately, then, everything comes down to a distinction between an event whose probability distribution is known (a proven risk needing to be prevented) and an event where the probability distribution is unknown, but where one can assign a known probability distribution to this unknown probability distribution (a "potential" risk warranting precaution). This distinction cannot stand up to scrutiny. No sooner has it been stated than it vanishes into thin air.

The ascription of probabilities to an unknown distribution of probabilities should remind us of the origins of modern decision theory more than fifty years ago, when the great statistician Leonard Savage, seeking to axiomatize rational behavior under uncertainty, introduced the concept of subjective probabilities.[8] The axioms Savage proposed had the virtue, like all good axioms, of appearing to be obvious. One of them says that, if a rational individual is indifferent between two lotteries, A and B, he is indifferent between either of these two lotteries and any linear combination of them.[9] Savage demonstrated that the behavior of an individual who acts in accordance with these axioms looks *as if* it were the solution to a maximization problem involving a function of gains and losses, called a utility function, and a set of numbers that can be interpreted as probabilities—as if, in other words, he were maximizing the mathematical expectation of his utility function, calculated with reference to the probabilities in question. These "personal" (Savage's term) or subjective probabilities do not correspond to any objective regularity of nature, only to a *consistency of choices* on the part of each person.

It will readily be seen that the introduction of subjective probabilities obliterates all the distinctions we have been considering up to this point, between uncertainty and risk, between risk of risk and risk, and between precaution and prevention. If a probability is unknown, one assigns a probability distribution to it "subjectively." No difference remains with the case in which objective probabilities are known at the outset. It becomes a matter of indifference to say:

1. We know with certainty (because our knowledge is rooted in the objectivity of observed frequencies) that X has a probability e of occurring; or
2. We attribute the subjective probability e to the hypothesis that the occurrence of X is certain (for, after all, $e \times 1 = 1 \times e$).

Uncertainty due to a lack of knowledge is thereby brought down to the same level as intrinsic uncertainty due to the unforeseeable character of a given event. Savage's triumph (in founding modern Bayesian statistical inference) turns out to be a Pyrrhic victory. It fatally undermines the very distinction that defenders of the precautionary principle would like to introduce between precaution and prevention. This point perfectly illustrates the universal ambition of rational choice theory. Because modelers of economic risk and insurance theorists neither see nor are capable of seeing any essential difference between prevention and precaution, they reduce the latter to the former.

Moreover, and independently of whatever weaknesses it may be thought to suffer from a philosophical point of view, Savage's version of this theory was found to entail technical difficulties that were to lead, if not to its abandonment, then at least to substantial revisions. Before examining one such modification, it will be well first to cast a critical eye on a related result that is generally numbered among the latest successes of neoclassical economics.

Acting without Waiting for Better Information

Earlier I recalled the German ancestry of the precautionary principle (*Vorsorgeprinzip*). As it happens, the precautionary principle also has an English line of descent, from the theory of saving, particularly in the form given it by Keynes. The great economist held that a "precautionary motive" is one of the main reasons why individuals do not consume all their income immediately, projecting themselves into the future and judging their present-day behavior from the perspective of their later self.[10] The theory of saving has been deepened and refined considerably since Keynes's time. Quite recently a team of French economists sought to apply some of his conclusions to the problem that concerns us here. Their analysis is extremely technical, and I will discuss here only one aspect of it, whose brilliance is all the more striking because of its paradoxical character.[11]

Let us consider two scenarios, in which the same economy is subject to identical exogenous risks but different kinds of information. In scenario A, the information available to agents about future dangers remains unchanged. In scenario B, the quality of information improves over time, thanks to advances in knowledge that are assumed to be independent of the decisions made by agents. The question then arises: in which scenario will the agents take preventive measures against risk sooner? One feels a strong temptation to reply at once that the answer is scenario A. In B, agents seemingly have an incentive to delay acting because they know that if they wait they will be better informed and hence able to prevent risks more effectively.

Despite its simplicity, this thought experiment does a good job of bringing out a surprising aspect of the precautionary principle, particularly in the form it assumes under the Barnier law: if it is necessary to act at once, it is not only *in spite* of the fact that one does not know enough, but *because* one does not know enough now and will know more later. A fine paradox—which the solution proposed by our French economists elegantly resolves. We are inclined to suppose it is better to wait in case B because postponing action reduces uncertainty. However, waiting also brings to bear a countervailing effect that works to increase uncertainty. In B, one anticipates having at one's disposal additional information at some time in the future, but obviously one cannot say exactly what that information will be. This point is essential. Our inability to predict the future state of knowledge is not a matter of practical difficulty, but instead runs up against a logical impossibility: if one could anticipate future knowledge now, it would be not future, but present knowledge. It follows that in case B, the measures that one will be led to take to ward off risk will depend on information that one does not currently possess. Before one has access to the information in question, the uncertainty should one wait to act will in fact be greater in case B than in case A, where the state of knowledge never changes and is therefore not itself subject to uncertainty.

These two effects work against each other, and the outcome depends on which one prevails. It is nevertheless demonstrated that under certain conditions the prospect of advances in knowledge will lead agents to take preventive action sooner than in the case that such progress is not expected. These conditions have two outstanding characteristics: first, they involve the psychology of agents in relation to risk, described in terms of their individual utility functions; second, their mathematical expression is so involved that a translation into ordinary language is scarcely possible.

No philosopher can be satisfied with this state of affairs. Insofar as the precautionary principle aspires to the status of an ethical rule, its justification cannot rest in the last analysis on a particular psychology, which moreover cannot be explained to the general public. Ethics is not a matter of preferences, a mere reflection of agents' inclinations. Without wishing at all costs to turn ethics into that cruel and forbidding thing that Kant was pleased to make of it, one cannot endow with any moral force imperatives that do no more than preface with the words "thou must" what agents are inclined to do in any case. Ethics in its true sense displays an *objectivity*, a *public character*,

Precaution, Between Risk and Uncertainty   71

and a *universality* that normative economic theory seems incapable even of mimicking, much less of providing a satisfactory basis for. Normative economics imagines that taking individual preferences as a foundation is democratic, but it ends up making ethics a question of taste.

Aversion to Uncertainty and the Evil Demon of Precaution

Savage's theory of utility gave rise to innumerable criticisms, some of which took the form of paradoxes.[12] A particularly elegant example, due to economist and strategic analyst Daniel Ellsberg (of Pentagon Papers fame) and based on an idea found in Knight's 1921 treatise,[13] has a direct bearing on the subject at hand.

Assume there are two urns. Urn *A* is transparent and contains ten black balls and ten white balls. Urn *B* is opaque and likewise contains twenty balls, black and white, although their proportions are unknown. One ball is drawn at random from each of the two urns. The player must do two things: first, choose one of the urns, and then bet on the color of the ball that is drawn. Savage's theory requires him to choose urn *B*, even though this choice places him in a position of uncertainty rather than of risk, to recall Knight's distinction. If the player is consistent, everything takes place as if he assigned subjective probabilities to the drawing of a black or white ball from urn *B*. One of two things will happen: if these probabilities are not 50–50, the player must prefer urn *B* to urn *A* and bet on what he expects to be the most probable color; if the probabilities are exactly 50–50, he will be indifferent between the two urns.

It seemed obvious to Ellsberg, however, that urn *A* should be chosen instead, because the probabilities in this case are objectively known. His intuition was confirmed by a poll he conducted with some of the leading decision theorists of the day, the vast majority of whom chose urn *A*. This is the Ellsberg paradox.

Almost thirty years later, economists Itzhak Gilboa and David Schmeidler revisited the enigma and proposed a weaker version of Savage's axioms that would favor the choice of urn *A* in the decision context that we have just considered.[14] To do this they introduced an element of "uncertainty aversion" (not to be confused with the familiar notion of risk aversion) whereby agents are assumed to prefer being able to rely on objective probabilities rather than having to formulate probabilities subjectively on the basis of insufficient information. This preference is already discernible in the model that we considered in the previous section. At first sight, Savage's axiomatics is not greatly altered by assuming the existence of an aversion to uncertainty; only the indifference axiom I mentioned earlier appears to be affected. Take two lotteries between which an agent is indifferent and mix them with known probabilities, thus forming a linear combination of the two lotteries with known weights. Savage's axiom, as we have seen, requires that the agent be indifferent between the new lottery and its two parents. In Gilboa and Schmeidler's scheme, by contrast, not only is the agent required not to have a strong preference for either one of the initial lotteries to the lottery created from them, he must slightly prefer this subsequent lottery to one of the other two. How does this change reflect an aversion to uncertainty? By starting out from two situations of uncertainty where probabilities may be known only imperfectly and then mixing them with known probabilities, one moves nearer to the domain of calculable risk. As it turns out, this apparently innocuous adjustment to Savage's axiom has profoundly unsettling implications for the standard conception of decision theory.

In effect, the revised axiomatics creates a situation in which the player begins by forming a priori not one, but a whole family of subjective probability distributions. For each of the possibilities of choice open to him, he then selects, within this family, the distribution that will minimize whatever gain he may hope to realize. Everything takes place as if there were an evil demon at his side who is capable of acting upon his mind. Each time the player is about to choose, he can count on his bad-luck companion to change his beliefs about the relevant probabilities for the worse. It is not too much to say that this evil demon perfectly embodies the spirit of precaution, at least as its modern theorists imagine it.

Let us now come back to the two-urn problem posed by Ellsberg. Suppose that the player begins by forming a family of subjective probability distributions with respect to urn B that lie in the interval between the case in which 45% of the balls are black and the case in which 55% are black. No sooner does the player consider betting on black than his evil demon makes him believe that the true proportion is 45%; but should he then be inclined to bet on white, the evil demon will cause him to change his mind and believe that 55% of the balls in urn *B* are black. Whatever bet the player may be ready to place regarding the ball that is about to be drawn from urn *B*, the chance of his winning is only 45%. Everything considered, then, he is better off choosing urn *A*.

This result has the virtue of agreeing with our intuitions. But it can be obtained only by introducing an ad hoc psychological assumption—aversion to uncertainty, which is to say a preference for situations in which objective probabilities are available. Even so, Gilboa and Schmeidler's analysis represents a considerable advance over the model that we examined in the previous section. Now, at least, the hypothesis is clearly stated in a way that lends itself to public debate. Nevertheless it suffers from a disabling weakness, for it has absolutely nothing to say about the range of the family of initial probability distributions. This essential element is left to be determined on other grounds. And yet the tendency of precaution to urge us, for every action we contemplate taking, to concentrate on the worst-case scenario, must be kept in check at all costs, lest it stray too far in the direction of catastrophism. Even Hans Jonas, as we have seen, insisted on this point. But on the crucial question of how far is too far, the present theory remains silent.

Still, from the philosopher's point of view, the revised theory subverts without fanfare the type of reasoning known since Aristotle as practical syllogism; or, more precisely, the version of this syllogism found in modern decision theory. It consists of a major premise: someone *desires X*; a minor premise: he *believes* that by doing *x* he will be able to obtain *X*; and a conclusion: if he is rational, he will decide to do *x* (or: it is rational for him to do *x*). The very structure of this syllogism assumes that the desires and beliefs *preexist* the decision and are independent of it. The revised theory, by contrast, introduces a retroactive feedback loop that, by seeming to reverse the course of time, if not actually to abolish it altogether, leads back from the decision being contemplated to what is supposed to determine it—in this case, beliefs. Philosophers of action have long been accustomed to treat beliefs (and desires) as at once causes of action and as reasons for action. But here both reasons and causes must be conceived as *following* the very thing of which they are the reasons and causes.

I doubt that economic theory can go much further than this in defining precaution in a way that would make it something new and different from the type of prudence that manifests itself in prevention.

CHAPTER 7

The Veil of Ignorance and Moral Luck

Beauty and the infinite wish to be seen unveiled.
—Victor Hugo, *A Postscript to My Life* (1901)

Decision theory, reformulated to avoid some of the paradoxes we have noted, leads to the strategy known as minimax, which consists in minimizing the maximum possible loss (or, in the "maximin" version that in principle is equivalent to it, in maximizing the minimum possible gain). Minimax was initially conceived in order to characterize the behavior of a player taking part in a game of chance who is infinitely cautious—one speaks in this case of an infinite aversion to *risk*—in the sense that he behaves as if the worst is always sure to happen.[1] It is very interesting to observe that an aversion to *uncertainty* will incline a player to adopt the same strategy. Everything takes place as if a player who prefers to reason on the basis of objective probabilities, rather than having to form them subjectively in response to insufficient information, behaves like an infinitely cautious player, in the sense given this notion by minimax strategy. The problem is that this still leaves us stranded on the hazardous terrain of subjectivity and psychology—a morass from which we must free ourselves at all costs if we are to supply ethics with a secure foundation in objectivity.[2]

In contemporary philosophical literature, a notable attempt to justify a minimax strategy exists that is wholly independent of psychology. This attempt is all the more interesting to consider in the context of the present discussion as it has been the object of repeated misinterpretations, particularly on the part of economists, who have sought to drag it back down to the level of psychology. I refer to the way in which John Rawls argues, in *A Theory of Justice*, for principles that are deliberately chosen in a situation of uncertainty, or what he aptly calls a "veil of ignorance."[3] Rawls's philosophy belongs to the deontological framework of Kantian morality. Its principal target is consequentialism, above all the utilitarian variant that has now dominated English-language philosophy for almost two centuries.

Let us imagine that the members of a society seek to determine the principles of justice that the basic structure of the social order must satisfy. If, as is ordinarily the case in the deliberative assemblies of a democratic society, each person brings to the debate a point of view that is shaped by his social and historical background and swayed by interests of class or status, and if he is prepared to use ruse or force to achieve the best possible outcome for himself in bargaining with his neighbors, it is plain that unanimous agreement will be impossible. But Rawls, as a good Kantian, holds that persons thus motivated and subservient to a diversity of specific determinants are not acting as free and rational individuals but as creatures belonging to an inferior order. Their deliberation therefore has no ethical value, being subject to the contingency of natural and social circumstances.

And yet the solution Rawls devises in order to make the social contract a *fair and equitable* collective act is very un-Kantian. He does not envisage severing the ethical domain from the purposes and interests of earthly existence. Kant held that it is enough that an act be inspired by a concern for the pleasure and happiness it gives, no matter how noble and elevated this act may be in other respects, to deprive it of any claim to moral standing as a result of its contamination by the sensible world of natural inclinations. Rawls's conception of disinterestedness, by contrast, requires neither saintliness nor absolute fidelity to an inhuman ideal.

The members of society will deliberate fairly, Rawls posits, so long as they have no access to information that would lead them, if they possessed it, to influence debate in a way that favors their personal advantage. He therefore imagines a hypothetical initial situation—what he calls the *original position*—in which each person is unaware not only of his place in society (knowing neither his social rank nor which class he belongs to) but also of his relative fortune with regard to intellectual and physical capacities, and even of his own psychological characteristics and preferences. Placed under this *veil of ignorance*, the members of society exercise judgment on an equal footing as free and rational persons. Nevertheless their motivations remain purely self-interested.

Since each person finds himself in exactly the same relation to his fellows as each of them does to him, agreement on the principles of justice that ought to govern the basic institutions of society cannot fail to be unanimous. Unanimity is therefore a logical necessity that follows from the conditions of the original position. Denied knowledge of anything that could set them against one another (their particular interests, their conceptions of the good life, and so on), they come to a decision, literally, as one. Economists who have read Rawls, believing themselves to be on familiar ground, suppose that this amounts to a classic decision problem—the problem confronting an isolated individual in a situation of non-probabilizable uncertainty who seeks to choose rationally. The author of *A Theory of Justice*, whose occasionally imprecise and ambiguous formulations are in some measure responsible for this interpretation, has more than once taken the opportunity to disavow it as a misreading. For he is concerned here not with a mechanism of the invisible-hand type, but with a social contract: the members of society talk to one another and make commitments to each other. Promises, pledges, and pacts are forms of ethical and political regulation wholly foreign to the world of *homo œconomicus* and crucial to the solution of the problems raised in *A Theory of Justice*. The unanimity Rawls imagines is therefore not of the sort that rational individuals deliberating in isolation from one another arrive at because each of them is faced with the same problem. It is the shared consent of autonomous and rational persons to the necessary implications of fairness.

Rawls aims to show that if this much is granted, agreement among the members of society will be reached on a set of specific principles of justice, carefully formulated and ranked. Note that Rawls does not claim to demonstrate that this represents the best possible outcome, the *optimum optimorum*. He contents himself with the more modest ambition of proving that, presented with a limited number of distinct conceptions of justice, among which figure the principles in question, the members of society will unanimously select the latter (the main rivals are various versions of utilitarianism).

Only one feature of these principles will occupy us here: the rational obligation they impose on members of society in the original position to adopt the point of view of those who, in the real world, will be the most disadvantaged among them. Rawls's conception of justice requires that the lot of the worst-off in various domains, carefully ranked, be maximized.

In response, a number of critics taxed Rawls with having given the members of his society an "infinite aversion to risk." Recognizing the good old maximin strategy from the theory of decision under uncertainty, these commentators believed themselves to be in familiar territory. Why, they asked, would all the members of society adopt this strategy? Why would they systematically identify with the plight of the least advantaged? Would not an inveterate poker player willingly run the risk of becoming a slave in exchange for the chance of becoming a king?

To be persuaded of the error of this objection, one has only to recall that *the psychology of the members of society has nothing to do with the matter, since they have no knowledge of their own preferences whatsoever.* Rawls's argument is of an entirely different sort. The members of his society are not isolated decision-makers; they jointly undertake to respect a contract whose principles are publicly defined and unanimously accepted. The contract creates obligations and imposes constraints. No one will agree to be bound by such a contract if he doubts his ability to honor his promise—all the more as this is permanent and irrevocable, and its object nothing less than the basic structure of society. If two conceptions of justice are in competition, and one of them makes possible, or even necessary, a position that is unacceptable to any member of society, whereas the other excludes such an eventuality, it is the latter conception that is to be preferred. Imagine that a person irrevocably committed himself, under a veil of ignorance, to certain basic principles, and that once the veil is pulled aside he finds himself in a position that, *as a consequence of the very form of social organization he has endorsed,* appears to him to be morally repugnant. This person would then be confronted with an insoluble and unbearable moral dilemma: either he repudiates a commitment that he himself deemed absolute, or he resigns himself to a state of affairs that he considers unacceptable, and in so doing forfeits all claim to dignity. What moral sentiment would he feel then? It is captured by the regretful exclamation: "Too late!"

The Veil of Ignorance and Moral Luck

Rawls's main purpose is to show that whoever occupies the least favorable position is condemned, in a society governed by utilitarian principles, to see himself as a mere means in the service of a greater end. No one can preserve his self-respect under these circumstances, for self-respect is nourished by the respect one is shown by others—which in this case is nonexistent. The Rawlsian scheme, by contrast, is designed to make the worst-off member of society no less a full-fledged citizen than anyone else, which, Rawls holds, is enough to prove its superiority.

This is not the place to examine in greater depth the arguments advanced by Rawls in defense of his thesis. The question that interests me here, in connection with our search for the proper philosophical stance to adopt in the face of new threats, is whether a "catastrophist" position—in the sense of the privilege granted to the worst-case scenario—can likewise be placed on more solid and universal foundations than a particular psychology with respect to uncertainty.

It will be useful at this juncture to introduce an idea from moral philosophy that to a neo-Kantian will sound like a contradiction in terms: the notion of "moral luck." This will permit us to gauge the extent of the chasm that separates even the most sophisticated forms of probabilistic judgment from moral judgment (or, quite simply, from rational judgment, provided that rationality is not confused with the singularly impoverished conception that economists have put forth under its name).

Let us suppose that two-thirds of the balls in an urn, like urn *A* of the Ellsberg paradox are black and the remaining one-third are white. Once again bets are placed on color. Obviously, one should bet that the first ball drawn will be black. The same goes for the second ball. Indeed, one should *always* bet on black, even though in a third of the cases on average, one may expect to be mistaken. Suppose that a white ball is drawn and we discover that we were mistaken. Will this result make us change our mind retrospectively about the rationality of the bet we made? No, of course not. We were still right to choose black, even if white happened to turn up in this instance. In the domain of gambling, at least, new information can have no conceivable retroactive effect on judgments as to the rationality of past decisions made under uncertainty or risk. As an analytic philosopher would put it, probabilistic judgment cannot in any way be supervenient, or dependent, on information that becomes available only after one has acted.

This limitation on probabilistic judgment has no counterpart in moral judgment. Suppose a man drinks heavily at a party one evening. Even though he knows he has had too much, he decides to drive home. It is raining, the road is wet, the light turns red, he slams on the brakes a little too late, and his car comes to a stop after a brief skid *beyond* the pedestrian crosswalk. Among the possible scenarios, consider these two: there was no one in the crosswalk, in which case he comes out of the experience with no more than a momentary fright; or he hits and kills a child. The law and morality, but especially morality, will treat the two cases differently. In a variant on this example, the man was sober when he got behind the wheel. He has nothing to reproach himself for. Yet he still may hit and kill a child, or else the crosswalk may be empty. Once again, either way, an unforeseeable outcome will have a retroactive influence on the judgment that both others and he himself pass on his conduct.

Then there is this example, due to the philosopher Bernard Williams,[4] which I shall simplify considerably. A painter—let us call him "Gauguin," for the sake of convenience—resolves to leave his wife and children and go to Tahiti, in the hope that the opportunity of leading a different life there will enable him to become the towering artist he aspires to be. Is he right to act in this way? Is it moral to do so? Williams argues with great sensitivity and subtlety that any possible justification can only be retrospective. Only the success or failure of Gauguin's endeavor will permit us—or him—to make a judgment. Yet whether or not Gauguin becomes a painter of genius is to some extent a matter of luck—the luck of being able to become what one hopes to be. When Gauguin comes to his painful decision to leave his family, he cannot know what the future holds in store for him. But to say that he is making a bet would be incredibly reductive. The concept of "moral luck," in its paradoxical aspect, fills a gap in our ability to describe what is at stake in this type of decision under uncertainty.

In France today, the law of both civil and criminal liability is subject to strong pressures to break with the principle of non-retroactivity in the context of new threats. That principle is enshrined in article 2 of the Civil Code, which stipulates: "The law provides only for the future; it has no retroactive effect." Under the influence of advances in science and technology, however, the landscape is shifting. Consider, for example, what is called development risk—the chance, as philosopher François Ewald puts it, that a product may have "an undetectable and unforeseeable defect, awareness of which manifests itself only after a certain lapse of time and imputation of which to the product or producer can be made only in another state of science than the one within which the product was marketed and used or consumed." Ewald's account of this dramatic new challenge to liability law takes on tragic overtones. As in Beethoven's Fifth Symphony, the theme of fate knocking on the door recurs like a leitmotif:

> The classic principle of civil liability, formulated in article 1382 of the Civil Code, which brought in the notion of fault, assumed that one is liable only for what one could have known, that one cannot be found liable without having been in a position to be aware of the harm caused. At that time one was judged and punished on the basis of what one had to have known, what one should have known, this being necessarily defined within the framework of a certain state of science and knowledge. The question posed by the hypothesis of development risk is new in the sense that it has to do with settling a sort of conflict of laws inside time. Can one fairly judge an act otherwise than with reference to the [understanding] of it [at the time of its performance]? Is it not unjust to judge an act with reference to another state of awareness than the one in which it was carried out? Is it just, even for purposes of compensating damages, to evaluate an act on the basis of suspicions and doubts that can only be formulated after the fact?
>
> It may be said that the problem of development risk confronts us anew with the workings of fate—but with the difference that, in the ancient world, fate was exclusively the province of the gods, whereas for us it is now always and necessarily associated with human agency. Our form of the tragic belongs to the world of technology, to those situations where, by virtue of transformations in awareness and in the nature of things themselves, the consumer discovers, in a sort of *retroactive revelation*, the harm that has befallen him, his disappointment, his misplaced confidence: "That was not what I believed, what I expected, what I was told, what I was promised"; and where the businessman, for his part, is sued for something that not only he did not and could not intend, but that he had done everything possible to avoid: "I did not do that, I did not intend for that to happen, I could not have intended for that to happen." The problem arises only in response to a new set of circumstances altering the relationship between

knowledge and power, and to the implications this has for liability; only as a result of the realization that modern societies are vulnerable to a new type of risk, with a new awareness of the tragic.[5]

All the elements that are needed to join up the veil of ignorance with the concept of moral luck are now to hand. Like Bernard Williams's Gauguin, but on an entirely different scale, humanity, considered as a collective subject, has chosen to develop its potential abilities in a way that brings it under the jurisdiction of moral luck. It may turn out that this decision will lead to great and irreversible catastrophes; it may turn out that humanity will find ways to avoid, circumvent, or get past them. No one can say what will happen. Any judgment is bound to be retrospective. Nevertheless, as in the case of collective deliberation analyzed by Rawls, it is possible not to anticipate the judgment itself, but to recognize beforehand that it can be arrived at only on the basis of what will be known once the veil has been lifted. *There is therefore still time* to ensure that those who come after us will never say: "Too late!"—a too late that would mean that they find themselves in a situation in which no human life worthy of the name is possible. And so we are, as Jonas writes, "tormented by a disinterested fear of what will occur long after us— more exactly, by a feeling of *anticipatory remorse* toward it."[6] It is therefore *the anticipation of the judgment's retroactive character* that founds and justifies the catastrophist stance.[7] In the third and final part of the present work, devoted to metaphysics, I shall come back to this remarkable loop that links the future with the past.

CHAPTER 8

Knowing Is Not Believing

Mine is a dizzying country in which the Lottery is a major
element of reality.

—Jorge Luis Borges, "The Lottery in Babylon"

Not all precaution theorists are like those risk economists and insurance experts who try to deal with new threats to the environment, health, and world peace by merely applying the usual tools of analysis with ever greater ingenuity. Many other theorists believe that the type of uncertainty associated with these threats is unprecedented, so that only by devising new tools, new conceptions of rationality, will it be possible to analyze and, in the best case, lessen it. New procedures of consultation, deliberation, and decision must be imagined that will make the anxiety that arises from uncertainty a shared burden that is borne equitably. If the sky threatens to fall upon our heads, should we not stand shoulder to shoulder and force governments to tell citizens the truth?

In the debate between risk economists and those who refuse to isolate decision-making from its social and political context, the strength of the economists' position derives from the fact that the novel character of the uncertainty associated with new threats is not immediately apparent. Why

83

84 Chapter 8

should it be necessary to abandon tried-and-true methods? Hazards are a fact of life from the point of view of the applied sciences and public policy. The engineer who calculates the diameter of a safety cable, the physician who prescribes a new drug, the manager of a nuclear power plant who tests a safety method at the risk of inadvertently provoking a fatal meltdown (as happened at Chernobyl), the head of state who imperils world peace by approving construction of an anti-missile shield to protect his country—all of them weigh pros and cons, reckon probabilities, and, whether they know it or not, do a "cost-benefit" analysis. What is there about the greenhouse effect, mad-cow disease, or industrial accidents that would justify proceeding otherwise?

We have already encountered one possible response. In the case of new threats, it is said, the uncertainty arises less from the existence of a particular risk than from the inadequacy of scientific knowledge. Uncertainty is not in the object, but in the knowing subject; it is not objective, but epistemic and subjective. That would be reassuring if it were true. One can bet that any "precautionary policy" will include the inevitable call for further research— as if the gap between what is known and what must be known could be filled by an additional effort on the part of the knowing subject. Unfortunately, however, there is no reason to believe that this is so. Once again it is Hans Jonas who best expressed the tragedy of our predicament:

> *Knowledge*, under these circumstances, becomes a prime duty beyond anything claimed for it heretofore, and the knowledge must be commensurate with the causal scale of our action. The fact that it *cannot* really be thus commensurate, that is, that the predictive knowledge falls behind the technical knowledge that nourishes our power to act, itself assumes ethical importance. The gap between the ability to foretell and the power to act creates a novel moral problem. With the latter so superior to the former, *recognition of ignorance* becomes the obverse of the duty to know and thus part of the ethics that must govern the ever more necessary self-policing of our outsized might.[1]

Jonas's position has the virtue of situating the question on the ethical level from the very outset. Our capacity for action having exceeded certain critical thresholds, we have an obligation to know that runs up against the impossibility of knowing. This situation therefore violates the meta-ethical principle that a duty to do something implies being able to do it ("'ought' implies 'can,'" in the jargon of philosophers). In general, there is no obligation to do what one cannot do. And yet in this case we *must* know, even though we cannot: "the knowledge called for," Jonas observes, "is *of necessity* always 'not yet' available, which means: [available] to foreknowledge never, and at best (if at all) to hindsight."[2] Many arguments might be advanced to anchor the unavoidable ignorance of which Jonas speaks in the *objectivity* of the systemic threats facing the world today. Three in particular deserve close attention.

The first concerns the complexity of ecosystems.[3] This complexity gives them both extraordinary stability and a resilience that is scarcely less remarkable. They can withstand assaults of all kinds and adapt in ways that will preserve their stability—though only up to a certain point. Beyond certain critical thresholds, as in the case of phase transitions in matter, they abruptly tip over into another state, collapsing completely or else forming other types of systems that may have extremely undesirable properties for human beings. In mathematics, such discontinuities are known as: catastrophes!

This sudden disappearance of resilience is a peculiar feature of ecosystems that no engineer could transpose into an artificial system without immediately losing his job. It means that the warning signals sound only when it is too late. So long as an ecosystem is far from reaching any critical threshold, it can be abused with utter impunity. A cost-benefit calculus will appear unnecessary because there are no visible costs. This is why humanity was able for centuries to pay no attention whatsoever to the environmental impact of its mode of development. As critical thresholds begin to be approached, however, cost-benefit calculations lose all point. The only thing that matters then is not crossing those thresholds. In either circumstance, economic calculation is of precious little value to us—and this for reasons having to do not with some temporary deficiency in our knowledge, but rather with the objective and structural properties of ecosystems. What is more, we do not even know where the critical thresholds are located.

The second argument concerns systems created by human ingenuity—technological systems, as we may call them—that interact with ecosystems to form hybrid systems. One of the major questions that is posed in this regard by industrial development is whether one can indefinitely substitute the artificial for the natural,[4] or, to use Illich's terms, heteronomous forms of production for autonomous ones. Technological systems exhibit quite different properties from ecosystems. This is a consequence of the crucial role played by positive feedback loops, which I have discussed at length in connection with technological evolution and von Foerster's theorem. Small fluctuations at the beginning of a system's life can be amplified and give it a direction that is wholly contingent and possibly catastrophic but which, experienced from within the system, takes on the semblance of fate. Obviously there is no way of predicting this type of dynamic or historical path. Here again, our lack of knowledge does not result from a state of the world that could be changed, but from a structural property: non-predictability is inherent in the functioning of the system.

Non-predictability is inherent for a third reason as well, this one of a logical nature, which we have already encountered and which Jonas describes as "the impossibility [of] predict[ing] future inventions, [for this] would amount to preinventing them."[5] Generally speaking, any forecast that depends on future knowledge is impossible, for the simple reason that to anticipate such knowledge would make it present, evicting it from its niche in the future.

Let me summarize the debate thus far. Precaution, in order to distinguish itself from prevention, is led to insist on the difference between the probabilizable uncertainty of risk (to which prevention corresponds) and uncertainty owing to a lack of knowledge (with which precaution is associated). In the first case, the uncertainty is objective; in the second, it is subjective. The theory of decision under uncertainty uses the concept of subjective probabilities to collapse these two levels into one. Everything becomes subjective, since both risks and the hypotheses made about them are assigned probabilities that reflect the consistency of an agent's choices rather than any external reality. It is clear why precaution theorists must protect their subject from domination by orthodox economists. Yet the analysis that I have just presented also tends to eliminate the difference between these two forms of uncertainty—but for exactly the opposite reason.

Why is uncertainty in relation to an event one deems *random*—a car accident, for example—considered an *objective* uncertainty, one that can be measured by means of probabilities? One might argue that this type of uncertainty is in reality just as subjective or epistemic. Historically, most European languages acquired their words for chance from the fall of a die.

But this physical phenomenon is today regarded as a deterministic system, albeit one that is extremely sensitive to initial conditions and therefore unpredictable—a "deterministic chaos," in current parlance. Nevertheless, the God whose existence Laplace famously thought it unnecessary to posit *would* be able to predict the face on which the die will land. Could we not therefore say that what is uncertain for us, but not for this mathematician-God, is uncertain only owing to our lack of knowledge, thus making it an epistemic and subjective uncertainty?

This conclusion is untenable. If a random event is unpredictable for us, that is not because of a lack of knowledge that could be remedied through more exhaustive research; it is because only an infinite being (or an infinitely powerful computing machine) could predict a future that our finiteness must forever prevent us from anticipating. Our finiteness is not a fact of the same order as the state of our knowledge. The former is an inescapable aspect of the human condition; the latter is a contingent fact, which could at any moment be different from what it is. We are therefore justified in treating the uncertainty of what is *to us* a random event as an objective uncertainty, even though that uncertainty may vanish for an infinite observer.

Our situation in relation to new threats, I maintain, is no different. There is something naive, not to say intellectually fraudulent, about making the application of the precautionary principle a function of "the absence of certainties, *given the present state of scientific and technological knowledge*," as the Barnier law does. I speak of fraudulence because this language suggests that with enough effort scientific research could overcome the uncertainty, which is assumed to be purely contingent.[6] The three arguments we have just examined show that the knowledge deficit in this case is no less structural than the one that prevents us from predicting a random event. Indeed, it is much more structural since, with regard both to the impact of human activity on ecosystems and to the development of technological systems, reliance on probabilities and statistical calculation can have no objective foundation in the absence of observable frequencies. Here probabilities can give us only a subjective, and therefore arbitrary, representation of an objective uncertainty. Precautionary theory strictly distinguishes between probabilizable risk and epistemic uncertainty: what does not come under the head of the one belongs to the other, and vice versa. But here we meet with a monster— an uncertainty that is neither epistemic (it is not in the head of the knowing subject) nor probabilizable (although objective, it cannot be reduced to statistics).

We do not know because we *cannot* know, being ourselves a part of natural and technological systems that we transform and which in turn transform us (a state of affairs that von Foerster's theorem represents in mathematical terms and whose implications it draws out). Such a non-epistemic and non-probabilizable uncertainty is very difficult to *manage*. Risk managers have no good way to "cover" it or "insure" against it. The precautionary principle as an analytical tool seems to be of no help either. One has only, as suggested earlier, to apply it to itself to see it become self-refuting. This gambit has largely been used by "reasonable" defenders of the precautionary principle to oppose the catastrophist conception of it, yet it can equally well be used to invalidate more moderate versions. Applying the principle to itself means, in the first place, asking whether the conditions for its application are satisfied. This leads to a fine paradox, since if they *are* satisfied—that is, if one is uncertain about the very existence of a grave and irreversible harm—then one cannot *know* that they are satisfied. It will be objected that when one is in doubt, one is well aware of being in doubt. That is true enough in the case of epistemic doubt. But I showed that in the cases that interest us, the uncertainty resides rather in the structural relationship that unites us with its object. One can easily be in a situation of uncertainty without knowing it. It not infrequently happens that scientists are mistaken in their certainty that a danger does not exist, when in fact it is objectively uncertain whether the danger exists or not. Wrongly believing themselves to live in a certain world, they do not know that their belief in a certain world is wrong.[7]

Where the uncertainty is such that the existence of uncertainty is itself uncertain, it is impossible to know whether the conditions for applying the precautionary principle are satisfied or not. If the precautionary principle is held to entail a reversal of the normal burden of proof, this element of undecidability is very awkward indeed. Innovators who are required to prove the harmlessness of a given product beyond any reasonable doubt, in the name of the precautionary principle, will always be able to insist that one first demonstrate that the principle actually applies in the case at hand—which is exactly what cannot be shown.

Applying the precautionary principle to itself also means focusing on the worst scenario that could result from its application. Precaution, especially in its "catastrophist" version, is itself a risky activity. It may, for example, block the introduction of new products that, although they may be dangerous, would be less dangerous than the ones they replace. If precaution aims to eliminate risk altogether, not only will it fail in this purpose; in the process it will use up scarce resources that would be better employed elsewhere, or prohibit because of its potential risks a vaccine that could have saved many lives. It is not hard to think of similar examples. If one takes into consideration the worst of these eventualities, one will probably be led to conclude that precaution argues against resorting to the precautionary principle. Returning to Jonas, the German philosopher Dieter Birnbacher draws the right conclusion from this type of reasoning: "Once one has crossed over into the realm of uncertainty, it no longer makes sense to weigh possible unknown disadvantages against possible unknown advantages. One reaches the point . . . where the heuristics of fear—a poor counselor in situations of risk in the strict sense—comes into force."[8]

I will not insist further on the fitting burial given the precautionary principle by some of those who had once advocated it.[9] One thing is certain at the conclusion of this debate: not much is left of the distinction between precaution and prevention. Nevertheless my initial question still awaits an answer, and all the more insistently as I have been unable to find one anywhere in the abundant literature on the precautionary principle.[10] What powerful motive prompted people one fine day to proclaim that we could not come to terms with the new threats facing us if we did not rid ourselves of our habitual analytical tools?

Only after much time spent poring over the thousands of pages written on the subject did I suddenly see what was right there before me, not hidden, but perfectly visible to the naked eye, like the purloined letter of Poe's tale hanging in plain sight from the mantelpiece. Neither uncertainty nor a lack of knowledge has anything to do with the matter.

It is hardly surprising that one should fail to grasp this right away. Arguments concerning precaution are made up of endless variations on the single, constantly repeated theme of uncertainty. And yet here and there a few false notes, which at first one is ready to overlook as nothing more than minor inconsistencies, point in another direction. Thus, for example, François Guery, discussing the difference between prevention and precaution, makes this startling claim: "At bottom precaution is not pure ignorance, but a quite verifiable suspicion, a virtual certainty."[11] Until then one had been under the impression that precaution was a response to *un*certainty, not certainty! Yet even the Kourilsky-Viney report, commissioned by the French government, feels obliged to dispel this misapprehension: "It is often thought that potential risks are improbable. They are unconsciously likened to proven risks whose probability is all the smaller in that they are well controlled. This is . . . inaccurate. . . . Potential risks, despite their hypothetical character, may have a high probability of coming to pass."[12] The jurist Marie-Angèle Hermitte makes a similar point about the concept of "theoretical possibility," which is supposed to describe a situation where the fragmentary evidence and data available to scientists prevents them from ruling out the hypothesis that a risk or danger exists. This is a crucial issue for legal scholars, since it involves determining whether a thought process—in the event, the formation of a hypothesis—can be regarded as a reflection or projection of a property of the real world. According to Mme Hermitte, the concept in question "means that a certain number of elements, interpreted in the light of preexisting knowledge and models, cause the thing to be possible, although there is no documented experimental proof of it. But that says nothing about the probable or improbable character of the event. And yet it is often taken by politicians, and sometimes by scientists consulted as experts, to mean that the probability is low. Jumping from the one concept to the other is inadmissible."[13]

A daunting uncertainty thus surrounds the threats that occupy our minds: are they very improbable or almost certain? They appear to us as both at the same time: very improbable, doubtless because we cannot imagine a catastrophe that is simultaneously of massive proportions and highly probable—the implausibility of the event compensates for the enormity of what is at stake—and yet also virtually certain, owing to the unmistakable air of fatality that hovers over such dangers. Of course, it is impossible for the same event to be at once very improbable and almost certain. This language betrays a modal confusion. Characterizing new threats as "almost certain" or "highly probable" is really a way of talking about the sense they are *ineluctable*—hence the recurring references to destiny and fate. Catastrophe is firmly engraved in our future, but with only a *low probability*. I will show that such an unprecedented configuration, far from entailing a pessimistic vision of our situation, may well be our only hope of salvation. By focusing our attention on this ineluctable event that, perhaps, will not come to pass, we will,

Knowing Is Not Believing

perhaps, find it within our power to act in such a way that the ineluctable does not in fact occur.

So far I have said nothing about the main obstacle that stands in our way. Let us grant that we are certain, or nearly so, that catastrophe awaits us, as the precautionary theorists' revealing slip suggests. The problem is that we do not *believe* it. We do not believe what we know to be the case. The challenge facing prudential calculation therefore has to do not with a lack of knowledge regarding catastrophe's indelible claim on our future, but with the fact that this claim is not credible.

Ever since Plato's *Theaetetus* and *Meno*, knowledge has been defined as justified, true belief. To know is to believe something that is true, and to believe it for sound reasons. If one knows p, then one necessarily believes that p is true. This theory of knowledge has been severely criticized in the twentieth century by analytic philosophers, who have produced a great many counterexamples. I shall not enter into this debate here. The temporality of catastrophes, in any case, refutes the implication that to know something is to believe it. We hold a catastrophe to be impossible even when the best information available to us obliges us also to hold that it is very probable, or even nearly or actually certain.

We should pause here to ask how governments behaved before the idea of precaution gained currency. Did they adopt policies aimed at *prevention*, which is to say the very thing that precaution seeks to improve upon? Not at all. They simply waited for catastrophe to strike before acting, as if its coming into existence was the sole factual basis on which its occurrence could legitimately be foreseen—too late, of course.[14] In its insistence that scientific uncertainty must not be allowed to delay the implementation of preventive policies, the precautionary principle completely mistakes the nature of the obstacle facing us. It is not uncertainty, scientific or otherwise, that stands in the way. It is the impossibility of believing that the worst will come to pass.[15]

The present situation is proof that a forecast of catastrophe produces no appreciable change either in the ways people act or in the ways they think. Even when their information is accurate, people do not believe what they know to be true. Of the horrors to come, Corinne Lepage remarks: "This is something that the mind rebels against, because one tells oneself that it is not possible."[16] With regard to global warming, in particular, she adds: "although for twenty years now we have *known perfectly well* the risk with which we are confronted, the truth of the matter is that we have done nothing what-soever."[17] In March 2001, President Bush cynically broke the promise he had made to the American people during his election campaign and announced that he would not press for a reduction of American greenhouse-gas emissions. The interests of the oil and coal industries carried the day. A similar observation may be made in the case of food safety regulation, among many others. Not only does the fear of impending disaster have no deterrent effect; not only does economic logic keep advancing like a steam roller; but no learning at all takes place.

The main obstacle, I repeat, is that the prospect of catastrophe is not credible. The fear of catastrophe fails to deter. The heuristics of fear is not a ready-made solution to the problem; it *is* the problem. I should not like to give the impression that it is chiefly a matter of psychology. Cognitive and affective elements do come into play, of course, which may be analyzed more or less perceptively. On the basis of an extensive sample of historical cases, the English economist David Fleming formulated an "inverse principle of risk evaluation," which states that a community's willingness to recognize the existence of risk depends on the degree to which it is convinced that solutions exist.[18] Philosophy of mind and cognitive psychology help us to explain in part, if not to justify, what otherwise appears to be wholly irratio-nal. Human beings are constantly revising their beliefs about the world in response to new information. This reorganization does not occur in a pas-sive way, for the knowing subject perpetually strives to maintain an overall consistency among his various beliefs. If he were to transform each new piece of information into a belief, he would risk having to call into question older beliefs, impregnably lodged in his mind, that form his view of the world and constitute his identity. All the relevant information at our disposal tells us that we cannot keep plowing ahead indefinitely, either in time or in space, with our present mode of development. But to question everything that we have come to identify with progress would have such staggering repercus-sions that we do not believe what we nonetheless know to be the case. There is no uncertainty here, or very little; at most there are excuses. Alas, uncer-tainty is not the obstacle.

The tragedy of September 11, 2001, showed in the most stunning way possible that knowledge is incapable of providing a foundation for credibil-ity.[19] It showed, too, that our capacity for imagining danger and mobilizing the appropriate emotions is no less impotent.[20] And yet, as I have noted, this is more than a question of psychology. It involves a whole metaphysics of temporality, as Bergson magnificently perceived in connection with artistic creation. The experience of our age now compels us to apply Bergson's lesson to the case of destruction. Creative evolution in human history has revealed its dark underbelly, *destructive evolution*.

In the chapters that make up the final part of this book I shall deal directly with the metaphysical problem, which until now I have only touched upon. First, however, it will be necessary to make one last detour through moral philosophy.

PART THREE

The Limits of Moral Philosophy and the Necessity of Metaphysics

The prophecy of doom is made to avert its coming, and it would be the height of injustice later to deride the "alarmists" because "it did not turn out so bad after all." To have been wrong may be their merit.

—Hans Jonas, *The Imperative of Responsibility*

Now the word of the Lord came to Jonah the son of Amittai, saying, "Arise, to Ninevah, that great city, and cry out against it; for their wickedness has come up before Me." But Jonah arose to flee to Tarshish from the presence of the Lord.

—Book of Jonah (1:1–3)

The future is inevitable and exact, but it may not happen. God lies in wait in the intervals.

—Jorge Luis Borges, "The Creation and P. H. Gosse"

CHAPTER 9

Memory of the Future

It is perfectly true, as philosophers say, that life can only be understood by looking back on the past. But they forget another proposition, no less true: that life can only be lived by projecting oneself into the future. And if one mulls over that proposition it becomes evident that life can never really be understood when one is immersed in time simply because at no particular moment can I find the necessary resting-place from which to look at my life in the only way that would make understanding possible— retrospectively.

—Søren Kierkegaard, *Journals* (1843)

Hans Jonas's *Imperative of Responsibility* so greatly extends the scope of our moral obligation, it has been said, that it annuls its own purpose by immobilizing us in dazed contemplation of catastrophes to come. Catherine Larrère, for example, holds that the "hyperbolic responsibility that emerges from Jonas's ethics deprives it of all capacity for indicating the precise actions to be undertaken, so that it amounts, in the extreme case, to an invitation to inaction."[1] It is true that Jonas's admonishments can sometimes be intimidating—for example, when he says that "a growing realm of collective action . . . by the enormity of its powers forces upon ethics a new dimension of responsibility never dreamed of before."[2] Nevertheless it can be shown that the view of his conception of responsibility as an incitement to inaction is utterly unfounded, and contrary to Jonas's own account of what it entails. First, however, I should like to examine how traditional moral doctrines conceive our responsibility in the face of a catastrophic future. It will be seen that these doctrines are vulnerable to the same criticism, if in fact it is a criticism at all.

In the 1970s English-language moral philosophy underwent a profound upheaval.[3] With the publication of Rawls's *A Theory of Justice* in 1971, the dominant position occupied by consequentialism for almost two centuries was suddenly challenged with astonishing force by the other great moral tradition, deontology. Until recently it seemed that the balance of power had decisively shifted under the influence of Rawls's work, and that consequentialism, particularly in its utilitarian version, had at least temporarily been consigned to the rubbish heap of outmoded philosophical ideas. Interestingly enough, it was in the context of a reflection on threats to the future of humanity that consequentialism reared its head once more, showing that it still had life left in it.

One of the leading representatives of the American consequentialist school, Samuel Scheffler, argued in an influential article that *if it is possible* to say where our responsibility lies in the present age, which he takes to be characterized by the globalization of threats, only consequentialism is capable of indicating the way forward.[4] Common-sense morality, he holds, is altogether inadequate to the task. Let me summarize his reasoning.

Common-sense morality is anchored—and this may explain why non-consequentialist elements occupy an important place in it—in a phenomenology of action that mirrors what has until recent times been the common historical experience of humanity. This experience made the following three propositions appear self-evident: a) positive actions are more important than omissions; b) immediate effects are much more visible, and therefore count for more, than long-term effects; c) individual effects carry greater weight than group, or composite, effects.

Two fundamentally non-consequentialist features of common-sense morality directly reflect this phenomenology of ordinary action. The first is

Memory of the Future

that negative duties ("Thou shalt not kill") have absolute priority over positive duties ("Help thy neighbor"). From the principle that what one does carries with it a greater responsibility than what one fails to do, it follows, for example, that one must not cause harm to an innocent person even if doing so is the only way to alleviate the suffering of ten others. The second feature is that we have special obligations toward family members and those closest to us that we do not have toward the rest of humanity.

This restrictive conception of normative responsibility, Scheffler argues, is wholly unsuited to our current predicament. Positive duties, he contends, have become as important as negative duties. For the consequentialist, the distinction between killing by means of an intentional individual act and killing because one cares only about one's own well-being as a citizen of a wealthy country while others die of hunger abroad is ever less tenable. We ought to care about *all* the consequences of our actions and not only those that are nearest and most visible to us. Hans Jonas, who was not a consequentialist, nevertheless concurred wholeheartedly with this opinion in contrasting the world we know today with the world of traditional morality in which "no one was held responsible for the unintended later effects of his well-intentioned, well-considered, and well-performed act. The short arm of human power did not call for a long arm of predictive knowledge."[5] Many of the threats that hang over our future are the result of a synergy among a multitude of minuscule individual actions, each of which, considered in isolation, has undetectable consequences (here one may think of climate change). The distinction between omission and action loses all meaning. If we abstain from driving to work for the sake of improving air quality, is that an omission? It is well and truly an action in the strongest sense of the word: an uncaused beginning, a setting in motion of something radically new in the web of human relations. Jonas called attention to this inordinate extension of the scope of action and its ethical implications: "Today human power and *its excess* by comparison with any certain knowledge of [its] consequences has taken on such dimensions that the simple daily exercise of our power, which constitutes the routine of modern civilization—and which we all perform—becomes an ethical problem."[6]

What made consequentialism inadequate in the sight of common-sense morality was that it attaches no importance, nor even any meaning, to distinctions that seem crucial to common sense. This weakness has now become its strength, to the point of clearing the field of all rivals, at least if we are to believe Scheffler. But the vaunted triumph of consequentialism is a Pyrrhic victory. The very same things that are held to demonstrate the necessity of resorting to it demonstrate its uselessness. The complexity of the causal chain that associates actions with consequences can be mastered neither on a practical nor a conceptual level (since models of complex phenomena must themselves be complex, exhibiting all the properties characteristic of such phenomena: sensitivity to initial conditions, unpredictability, and so on). It does away with any hope of calculating consequences. This fact, which made implementing the precautionary principle an exercise in self-contradiction, is equally fatal to consequentialism. Jonas was quite aware of this. "The extension of power is also the extension of its effects in the *future*," he observed. "From which it follows: we can *exercise* the increased responsibility that we *have* in each case, willingly or unwillingly, only on the condition of proportionately increasing our prediction of consequences as well. Ideally, the extent of prediction should equal the length of the chain of consequences. But such knowledge of the future is impossible."[7]

Scheffler's reasoning leads to a desperate conclusion. If the consequentialist stance is no better adapted to the present situation than a normative conception of responsibility based on common-sense morality, then the very notion of responsibility ends up appearing to be without foundation, at least on the ethical level.

The misfortune of consequentialism in advertising itself as the sole path to salvation, only to be forced to admit its own powerlessness, is not peculiar to it. The extreme form of Kantian morality promoted by Sartre under the name of existentialism experienced the same fate. His lecture on existentialism as a humanism, delivered in October 1945—and therefore *after* the catastrophe of the war, not before it—considered the task facing European nations of constructing out of the rubble something resembling human society. Citing the essayist and poet Francis Ponge's dictum "Man is the future of man," Sartre commented: "This is absolutely true. However, if we were to interpret this to mean that such a future is inscribed in heaven, and that God knows what it is, that would be false, for then it would no longer even be a future. If, on the other hand, it means that whatever man may appear to be, there is a future waiting to be created—a virgin future—then the saying is true. But in that case we are abandoned"—that is, condemned to freedom. This freedom makes extraordinary demands on the individual: "I am constantly compelled to perform exemplary deeds. Everything happens to every man *as if* the entire human race were staring at him and measuring [it]self by what he does." The existentialist preoccupation with a sense of personal anguish arises from the belief that "a man who commits himself, and who realizes that he is not only the individual that he chooses to be, but also a legislator choosing at the same time what humanity as a whole should be, cannot help but be aware of *his own full and profound responsibility.*" Any doubts one might still have about the Kantian inspiration of these remarks are dispelled once and for all by the following passage: "Certainly, many believe that their actions involve no one but themselves, and were we to ask them, 'But what if everyone acted that way?' they would shrug their shoulders and reply, 'But everyone does *not* act that way.' In truth, however, one should always ask oneself, 'What would happen if everyone did what I am doing?' The only way to evade that disturbing thought is through some kind of bad faith."[8]

This, then, is where Kant's injunction—"Act only according to that maxim whereby you can, at the same time, will that it should become a universal law"—leads when it is pushed to its logical conclusion. Sartre's insistence on behaving "as if the entire human race were staring" at one's every action brings to mind a characteristic trait of incipient psychosis.[9] Indeed, the link between Kantian doctrine and madness has not gone unremarked.

But if neither consequentialism nor deontology will do, what alternative is left to us? Perhaps it will be necessary after all to take seriously the heuristics of fear that Jonas proposed, as well as the ethics of the future (*Zukunft*) that accompanies it.

Jonas's ethics is not consequentialist. The reason for this will become clearer in due course. At the deepest level, it has to do with the direction of time. Consequentialism proceeds from the present toward the future, as the etymology of the word "consequence" clearly indicates: that which goes with while coming after. The ethics of the future is not the one that will prevail, or should prevail, in the future; it is the one that takes shape when one looks at the present, our present, from the vantage point of the future. It is this reversal on the metaphysical level that accounts for the specificity, originality, and beauty of the ethics that Jonas elaborates. Consider what he has to say in this connection about the heuristics of fear: "What can serve as a compass? The anticipation of the threat itself! It is only in the first glimmer of its tumult *that comes to us from the future*, in the dawn of its planetary scope and in the depth of its human implications, that we can discover the ethical principles from which the new obligations corresponding to our new power can be deduced."[10] Later I shall come back to the marvelous enigma of a signal that comes to us from the future—as if we were to find in ourselves, in the deepest recess of our memory, a trace of the catastrophe that has yet to occur. In a sense it is this miracle that every prophecy performs, even ones as mundane as the putatively scientific prediction made by a government agency regarding the future state of the economy.

That Jonas's ethics is not Kantian is much easier to see, since he is at pains to make this point himself in discussing the crucial metaphysical question: is the future that we say we foresee the future *tout court*—an actuality yet to come, of course, but actual nonetheless—or is it instead a conditional future, a hypothetical, counterfactual future, a future of what would happen if . . . ? Jonas is quite explicit:

> Kant's categorical imperative . . . enjoined each of us to consider what would happen *if* the maxim of my present action were made, or at this moment already were, the principle of a universal legislation; the self-consistency or inconsistency of such a *hypothetical* universalization is made the test for my *private* choice. But it was no part of the reasoning that there is any probability of my private choice in fact becoming universal law, or that it might contribute to its becoming that. Indeed, *real* consequences are not considered at all, and the principle is one not of objective responsibility but of the subjective quality of my self-determination. The new imperative [that I have proposed] invokes a different consistency: not that of the act with itself, but of its eventual *effects* with the continuance of human agency in times to come. And the "universalization" it contemplates is by no means hypothetical—that is, a purely logical transference from the individual "me" to an imaginary, causally unrelated "all" ("*if* everybody acted like that"); on the contrary, the actions subject to the new imperative—actions of the collective whole—have their universal reference in their actual scope of efficacy: they "totalize" themselves in the progress of their momentum and thus are bound to terminate in shaping the universal dispensation of things. This adds a *time* horizon to the moral calculus which is entirely absent from the instantaneous logical operation of the Kantian impera-

tive: whereas the latter extrapolates into an ever-present order of abstract compatibility, our imperative extrapolates into a *predictable real future* as the *open-ended* dimension of our responsibility.[11]

The fact that our power to act outstrips our capacity to foresee the consequences of our actions both imposes upon us the moral obligation to predict the future and prevents us from satisfying it. To escape this difficulty, Jonas from the outset places himself in the future, which is to say at the momentarily fixed endpoint of a continuous and ever-changing history.[12] It is as if time were frozen in a loop that connects the present with the future and the future with the present. I shall now try to demonstrate the logical consistency of this metaphysical gambit and to show that it alone can circumvent the obstacle that keeps us from coming to terms with the time of catastrophes—not uncertainty, but our failure to believe that disaster will strike.

CHAPTER 10

Predicting the Future in Order to Change It (Jonah vs. Jonas)

What moved Bergson, what never ceased to move him, was the very simple fact that there was something new at every moment of his life, the very general fact that there is something new at every moment wherever there is life. This novelty, it should be stressed, is the radically new, which is what is meant by the word "unpredictable." It is therefore not a pseudo-novelty that was potential before being actual, that was there, hidden, before appearing, that was unpredictable only because our understanding does not have the power to see it. No limitation of the mind is involved; the emotion Bergson felt arose from the fullness of existence: the joining of being and time.

—Henri Gouhier, introduction to Bergson's Œuvres (1959)

So far I have established that precaution is self-refuting in the worst case, and, in the best case, indistinguishable from prevention. As for prevention, its failure to foresee catastrophe, and therefore to prevent it, is rooted in the metaphysics we spontaneously embrace in the face of a new event that ushers in a temporal discontinuity—especially an event

105

whose anticipation, were we to take it seriously, would fill us with horror. As Bergson understood through his own personal experience, the crucial feature of this spontaneous metaphysics is that an event's possibility does not precede the moment when it bursts forth into time. Since a catastrophe does not enter the realm of the possible before it occurs, it cannot be anticipated; one does not project oneself into it. This metaphysics makes prevention impossible. The characteristic feature of prevention is that an event that is prevented from happening is thereby relegated to a world of unactualized possibilities. In the metaphysics that underlies prevention, possibilities preexist the realization of one among their number, and those that fail to be actualized survive forever in a limbo populated by all those things that might have been but were not. Every threat that succeeds in deterring an adversary, for example, leaves behind in its wake the unactualized possibility that it could have been carried out. If the United States had heeded the urgings of John von Neumann and Bertrand Russell in the immediate aftermath of World War II, it would have waged preventive war against the Soviet Union by leveling it under a wave of hydrogen bombs. The United States did not do this, and it may be that the perception that it could have done so contributed to world peace. In the metaphysics of prevention, that possibility of nuclear destruction remains in any event a possibility forever, not in the sense that it could still today be realized, but in the sense that it will forever remain the case that it could have been realized.

Decision theorists and adepts of rational choice feel at home with this traditional metaphysics, whose origins may be traced back to Leibniz. What Leibniz said about God, decision theorists say about mankind. Contemplating the whole set of possibilities, the divine or human decision-maker chooses and brings into existence the one that maximizes a certain magnitude or value. All of these possibilities are conceived as being fully present before the choice is made and living on afterward. By rejecting this tenet of traditional metaphysics, Bergson makes prevention an apparently impossible task.

No one believes in the possibility of disaster until it has struck. Because we react only to the actuality of disaster, we react too late. There is nevertheless in traditional metaphysics a concept that may offer us a way out of this impasse. The catastrophe lies ahead of us; its habitat is the future. If we could make the future real, give it the same actuality as the present, that might just do the trick.[1] This is precisely what the metaphysical principle of the reality of the future tries to accomplish. It may be expressed very simply. It proceeds by assigning a value, true or false, to propositions about a future event before time has had a chance to decide.[2] Whenever we use the future indicative to assert something—for example, "The World Trade Center towers will be rebuilt before the end of the century"—we presuppose the reality of the future. As a matter of linguistic convention, the proposition we assert by this sentence is true at the moment that we utter it if, and only if, it *will in fact be* true, before the end of the century, that the towers of the World Trade Center have been rebuilt. Each time that we make a prediction, then, we credit the future with an actual existence.[3] It would be a gross error, however, to conclude that this attitude necessarily amounts to fatalism. To say that the future is already in some sense what it will be does not mean that it could not be different from what it will be.

But we will not be able to extricate ourselves from the difficulty so easily. Suppose that we succeed in preventing a catastrophe. In traditional metaphysics, the catastrophe is thereby consigned to an unactualized possible world and so loses its place in the actual future, the only future that we have. Deprived of its reality, it also loses its power to make us react. In Bergson's metaphysics, the situation would be still worse since the catastrophe, having failed to become actual, would never enter into the realm of possibility.

I will show that to overcome or at least to find a way around the obstacle, it will be necessary to engrave the catastrophe in the future much more radically by making it *ineluctable*. We shall then be able to say in all honesty that we act to prevent it *thanks to the memory that we have of it*. Metaphysical argumentation will give existence and meaning to those signals of which Jonas speaks that, heedless of the laws of physics, reach us from the future.

Here, unmistakably, we find ourselves in the realm of paradox. It will be objected that I have hardened the metaphysical status of the impending catastrophe so that not only shall it come to pass but, once it has occurred, it will appear that it could not have *not* occurred. Am I really suggesting that this is the way not only to believe in the reality of the catastrophe, but to find at last the resolve needed to prevent it? But if the disaster is prevented, how can it be said to have been ineluctable? The contradiction seems to verge upon the absurd. Bergson's argument, which I recalled in the prologue, suggests a way of resolving it, however. The metaphysics that I am about to develop is not

Bergson's; indeed, in the case of destructive evolution, it is in a sense the anti-dote to Bergson's metaphysics. Nevertheless mine shares with his a crucial feature, namely, that the truth values of modal propositions (concerning the possible, the necessary, and so on) are adjusted, or revised, over time. Recall that according to Bergson, speaking of the sudden emergence of something utterly new in the form of a work of art, before the event occurred it was not possible, but with the event's occurrence it becomes true that it will always have been possible. Its possibility, Bergson says, does not precede its reality, but will have preceded it once the reality has appeared. We, in turn, will have to accustom ourselves to the idea that once a catastrophe has occurred, it was impossible for it not to occur, but that before it occurs it was possible that it might not occur. It is in this interval that our freedom to act finds a toehold.

The activity of prediction may show us a way out. Making predictions is one of the essential purposes of science: astronomers forecast the next lunar eclipse, meteorologists tomorrow's weather, economists movements in share prices, geologists the threat of earthquakes. Obviously no physical law is violated in doing these things; there is no signal that travels backward in time from the future to the present. All such predictions are made on the basis of an idealized model that simulates through mathematical deduction the chain of causes and effects operating in the real world. This kind of deduction exists outside of the time in which physical phenomena unfold. Indeed, one might say that in making the future the contemporary of the present, it signs time's death-warrant. The scientist, no less than the poet, has managed to master the passing of time: what the poet achieves through the act of writing, the scientist obtains by substituting for reality an image of reality—a model that both imitates and demands to be imitated. The invention of complex models fatally undermined this ideal, since, as we have seen, the properties of a complex model cannot be *deduced* from knowledge of the model itself. It is only through *simulation*—this time in the sense that the word has come to acquire in computer science—of the model's behavior on a computer that its properties are revealed, thus restoring to time some measure of its power to generate the radical novelty of new events.

There is nothing paradoxical about the activity of prediction itself. However, human beings do not make predictions solely in order to know the future; they make them also in order to act upon the world. Predictions are made in the image of God, or at least of the one imagined by theologians and philosophers, who is both prescient—He knows at every moment the truth-value of propositions concerning future events—and providential—He intervenes in human affairs. For human beings, the importance of anticipating catastrophes is bound up with a desire to prevent them. This is where the paradox comes in.

The existence of false predictions is not a problem in and of itself. Every day, both individually and collectively, we make predictions that are not borne out by events: unaware that a strike is about to be declared, I expect my plane to leave at the scheduled time; owing to developments it cannot anticipate, the government forecasts a rate of economic growth for the coming year that may turn out to be only half that much. The cases that I wish to consider are very different. They include, on the one hand, predictions that are false only because they have been made, and, on the other hand, *predictions made so that they will not come true.* These two distinctive configurations pit against one another two professional prophets who, by an irony of fate, bear the same name: Jonah, the biblical prophet of the eighth century B.C. mentioned in the second Book of Kings, and Jonas, the German philosopher of the twentieth century.

In the Book of Jonah (1:1–3), we read this: "Now the word of the Lord came to Jonah the son of Amittai, saying, 'Arise, go to Nineveh, that great city, and cry out against it; for their wickedness has come up before Me.' But Jonah arose to flee to Tarshish from the presence of the Lord."[4] Yahweh commands Jonah to prophesy the fall of Nineveh, which has sinned against Him. Instead of obeying, Jonah shirks the prophet's task and flees. Why? We are not told. Everyone knows what happens next: Jonah's boarding of a ship bound for the Strait of Gibraltar, the raging storm that churns up the seas, the casting of lots that reveals Jonah's responsibility for placing the lives of the ship's crew in danger, his being thrown overboard by the sailors in order to calm the wrath of the Lord, the great fish that mercifully swallows him and finally, after three days and three nights have passed, vomits him onto dry land. But does anyone remember the end of the story? It is only then that we understand why Jonah rebelled against his God. It was because he had foreseen, able prophet that he was, what would happen if he were to issue his prophecy! What would have happened is what now does in fact happen. Yahweh once again orders him to prophesy the fall of Nineveh. This time, having been made to understand the price of disobedience, he obeys. The people of Nineveh repent, convert, and receive God's pardon. Their city is spared. But for Jonah it is a bitter humiliation. The biblical text tells us that it leaves him "angry."

Although Jonah figures among the minor prophets, and although the Book of Jonah seems to have no basis in historical fact, his story has a quite singular importance for both Jews and Christians. Orthodox Judaism has never attributed to the prophets the central role ascribed to them by Christianity. The exegetical commentaries known as *midrashim* pay them relatively little attention. An exception is the Book of Jonah, regularly used in Hebrew liturgy and particularly on Yom Kippur, the day of atonement in which it occupies a central place. And Christians will recall that when Jesus is summoned to give a sign that will manifest his true identity, he answers, "No sign will be given to [you] except the sign of the prophet Jonah" (Matthew 12:38–42 and 16:1–4; Luke 11:29–32). Plainly Jonah is a unique figure. We must try to understand why.

Let us begin with the chagrin felt by Jonah. I am not a specialist in such matters. Nevertheless I venture to supplement the traditional understanding of Jonah's attitude with a conjecture suggested to me by my work on doomsaying. The conflict between Yahweh and Jonah is the result, we are told, of the fact that Jonah does not wish that the Ninevites be saved. Nineveh was the capital of the Assyrians, and would remain so until 612 B.C. The Israelites regarded the Assyrians as the fiercest and most barbaric of their enemies. Jonah knows that the Lord's wrath, which he is ordered to communicate to the Ninevites, will bring about their repentance and their pardon. Jonah loves his people, and does not wish to see them destroyed by a savage foe. The Lord loves the Israelites, too, but He also loves Nineveh, and Jonah knows it—although Yahweh will tell him so only at the end, when Jonah is made to feel ashamed for showing pity for a plant and surprise that God should feel compassion for human beings. Torn between loyalty to his people and obedience to God, Jonah chooses to flee.[5]

Jonah's dilemma is therefore a moral one. I contend that it is also metaphysical. While not all commentators agree, it seems to me that the essence of biblical prophecy is its concern with prediction.[6] To be sure, the prophets were not alone in claiming to foretell the future. They were surrounded by a whole cohort of sorcerers, soothsayers, astrologers, necromancers, magicians, enchanters, and others of that ilk whose feats, though forbidden,[7] were not easily distinguishable from those of true prophets. It is precisely in order to differentiate prophets from charlatans that emphasis is laid on the fact that a prophet is also, or above all, one who *proclaims* and *interprets* the word of God.[8] But Deuteronomy (18:21–22) makes it clear that the sole criterion for recognizing a true prophet is that his words come true—that his prophecy proves to be accurate: "And if you say in your heart, 'How shall we know the word which the Lord has not spoken?'—when a prophet speaks in the name of the Lord, *if the thing does not happen or come to pass, that is the thing the Lord has not spoken*; the prophet has spoken it presumptuously; you shall not be afraid of him." In other words, the non-realization of a prophecy proves that it is not of divine origin. This is not a very useful criterion, since there is no other way to determine whether the prophecy was a genuine prophecy than to wait and see if it is actually borne out by events. Only the future can decide. Here we find ourselves confronted once more with the logical impasse of catastrophism: the prophet of doom will be taken seriously and set apart from mere charlatans only when the predicted disaster occurs—by which point it will be too late.

It is in this light that Jonah's metaphysical dilemma must be understood as one of the sources of his anger. Jonah knows that his prophecy, in acting upon the world—*by virtue of the very fact of its acting upon the world*—will become false. How, then, could he not resent his treatment at the hands of the Lord, who has set a trap for him in that labyrinth we call time? If he assumes the prophet's task and thereby accomplishes the result God intended by averting the fall of Nineveh, he will be transformed into one of those conjurors and charlatans who are an "abomination" in the sight of the Lord (Deuteronomy 18:11–12).

The question arises whether Jonah might have avoided the whole dilemma if, rather than fleeing, he reasoned thus: "My prophecy asserts what would in fact happen *if* I did not make the prophesy." Let us imagine that Jonah does *not* hope that Nineveh will fall. He will then become aware of having an extraordinary power to ensure that this will not occur, namely, by predicting that it will occur. This is what is called *prevention*: the announcement of an impending catastrophe succeeds in preventing its occurrence. We know that God does not in fact wish for Nineveh to be destroyed. Can Jonah, for his part, evade his metaphysical dilemma in like fashion? Certainly not, for he cannot logically conflate the future as it will occur—our future, the future of our world—with a conditional future, which is therefore not a future at all, but simply a hypothesis about what would have happened if Jonah, who prophesies catastrophe, had not prophesied it.

Let us now leap over twenty-eight centuries in a single bound and look at the way in which the German philosopher Hans Jonas conceived of his task as a prophet of doom at the end of the second millennium. "The prophecy of doom is made to avert its coming," Jonas says in words I have quoted as an epigraph to the present part of this book, "and it would be the height of injustice later to deride the 'alarmists' because 'it did not turn out so bad after all.' To have been wrong may be their merit."[9]

The contrast is evident: Hans Jonas rejoices at the very thing that his illustrious predecessor considered to be an insuperable dilemma. Jonas is like God in the Book of Jonah: he prophesies the future—causes it to be prophesied, in God's case—for the express purpose of ensuring that it will not occur. And here the future does in fact mean the future, the future in its actuality—what is really going to happen. The long passage that I quoted in the previous chapter, in which Jonas dissents from Kant's categorical imperative, makes just this point. Jonas is not interested in hypothetical futures, which, as I have said, are not futures at all.

The problem is that, from the perspective of our traditional metaphysics, "predicting the future in order to change it" is a logical impossibility. Admittedly, this problem does not stop people from going blithely about their business. With the approach of the year 2000, a popular science magazine asked twenty or so professional forecasters, from neighborhood fortune-tellers to macroeconomic modelers, why it was so important to predict the future. The majority replied: so that we can change it.

Metaphysics, it should be kept in mind, is a rational discipline. There are truths in metaphysics; or, more precisely, given a consistent metaphysical system, the propositions expressed within its framework possess a truth value, which is to say they are either true or false. In the metaphysics that I call "traditional," and which I have identified with the name of Leibniz, it is true to say that the future is no less unalterable than the past. David K. Lewis, probably the greatest metaphysical logician of the twentieth century and, after his fashion, an heir to Leibniz, expressed this truth in the following terms, in which the mood and tense of the verbs have a crucial importance:

What we *can* do by way of "changing the future" (so to speak) is to bring it about that the future is the way it actually will be, rather than any of the other ways it would have been if we acted differently in the present. That is something like change. We make a difference. But it is not literally change, since the difference we make is between actuality and other possibilities, not between successive actualities. The literal truth is just that the future depends *counterfactually* on the present. It depends, partly, on what we do now.[10]

The concept of counterfactual dependence requires explanation, for it will figure prominently in what I have to say next. A conditional proposition of the "if p then q" type may be indicative ("If it rains tomorrow, I will not go to work") or counterfactual ("If I were younger, I would run in the New York Marathon"). The term "counterfactual" refers here to the presence of an antecedent ("If I were younger") that is contrary to fact (alas, I am not younger than I am). The way these two types of conditionals behave in our reasoning is not at all the same. To take a classic example, the proposition "If Shakespeare did not write *Troilus and Cressida*, someone else did" is indubitably true since the play exists, and so it must have an author. By contrast, to assert the truth of the counterfactual proposition "If Shakespeare had not written *Troilus and Cressida*, someone else would have," is highly problematic—especially for those who believe that only the Bard could have produced a masterpiece of this order.

To say that the future depends counterfactually on the present is simply to regard as true a whole series of propositions of the type: "If I had done this, whereas in fact I did something else, the future would (or might) be different." In that case we would find ourselves in another world, no less possible than the one we know, but not actualized. This is what makes us suppose that we can change the future. But in our world the future is simply what it is, or, rather, it is what it will be. There is nothing I can do between now and any particular moment in the future in question that could justify the indicative conditional proposition: *if I do this, then that future will be different.*

The task that Hans Jonas set for himself seems therefore to be a logical and metaphysical impossibility. Unless, of course, we can demonstrate that there exists another metaphysics of time and free will, different from but every bit as consistent as the one that seems to us so natural that we do not even pause to think about it. Jorge Luis Borges, the greatest metaphysical poet of modern times, shows us a path with a remark that I placed along with the quotation from Jonas at the head of this third and final part of the present work: "The future is inevitable and exact, but it may not happen."[11] If this is the solution, it has the form of a new paradox. Much work remains to be done to elucidate it. Borges goes on to say that God stands watch in the "intervals." Here we need to replace God by mankind: the responsibility of vigilance lies with us alone. Whereas the biblical prophet Jonah's metaphysical dilemma demonstrates the pitfalls of prevention as traditionally conceived, the German philosopher Jonas points to a way out. Provided that Hans Jonas's metaphysics can be given a solidity that it does not yet attain in his own writings, we may build on it to develop a rational and coherent theory of doomsaying.

CHAPTER 11

Projected Time and Occurring Time

What is an infinite intelligence? the reader may ask. All theologians define it; I prefer to give an example. The steps a man takes, from the day of his birth to the day of his death, trace an inconceivable figure in time. The Divine Intelligence perceives that figure at once, as man's intelligence perceives a triangle. That figure (perhaps) has its determined function in the economy of the universe.

—Jorge Luis Borges, "The Mirror of the Enigmas"

Are these the shadows of the things that Will be or are they shadows of the things that May be, only?

—Charles Dickens, *A Christmas Carol*

Predicting the future obviously does not mean succumbing to fatalism. Nevertheless the difficulties involved in taking the predicted future as a guide for present action cannot be underestimated; indeed, they have been well known since antiquity. After consulting the oracle, the heroes of Greek tragedy discover that their futile efforts to escape its verdict only hasten its fulfillment. In our own time, individual investors acting on the basis of official economic forecasts may find that the aggregate effect of their decisions brings about something quite different from what was predicted.

Let us imagine a situation where we know that our prediction will influence events, and so we must take its consequences into account if the future is to confirm what we have predicted. This is one of three possible cases of prediction in human affairs. The first involves foreseeing the state of a system that is indifferent to our perceptions of it, a wheat harvest in a remote country, say, or the state of automobile traffic in a foreign city. Here the task is akin to predicting the future state of a physical system, and modeling is the appropriate method. The second case is not strictly speaking a prediction at all, but a speech act, which sometimes takes the form of a threat or promise and is expressed by conditional propositions of the type: "This is what would happen if you were to make such-and-such a decision, or if I were to do such-and-such a thing." Jonah's prophecy in the Bible comes under this head: the best he can do is to prophecy what would have happened if he had not made his prophecy. The third case is the one I wish to consider here.

It is hard to imagine an election held today without polls preceding it and announcing its results in advance, sometimes with such precision that voters wonder, not without a certain annoyance, what use it is to go to the trouble of voting. In the 1950s, Herbert Simon, a future Nobel laureate in economics and one of the founders of artificial intelligence, argued that there is no difference in principle between the social and the natural sciences as far as the possibility of making exact predictions is concerned. Simon was objecting not to the claim that in the social sciences observation and forecasting are more difficult, but to the claim that they hopelessly disturb the system that is being observed. The prediction of a social phenomenon, once known and publicly advertised, is bound to modify the event in question. A poll, for example, by making the state of public opinion known to the public, alters this very state. When a new poll is taken, some respondents may follow the crowd and prefer the winner of the earlier poll; others, as Montesquieu long ago suggested, may try to redress the balance by throwing their support behind the underdog. It is in order to avoid such effects that the announcement of poll results was long prohibited in France in the days just before an election.

Simon claimed to refute this argument. He showed that the process described above will converge on a "fixed point," that is, a state of opinion that remains stable when the public is informed of it.[1] The problem is that Simon did more than this: he showed that there are generally several fixed points. This means that if a polling organization wished to play Nostradamus by deliberately making its prediction coincide with such a fixed point, it would possess an exorbitant power to manipulate public opinion by choosing one fixed point over another. Notice, however, that this power is no less great if, as seems reasonable, pollsters simply inform the public of the "raw" state of opinion as it stands before the results are announced. Assuming that the pollsters know how public opinion will react to the information regarding its own state, choosing not to take this knowledge into account under the pretense of objectivity also shapes the development of opinion in a given direction. The possibility arises, then, that the publication of polls, by condemning them to lack either accuracy or neutrality, makes it impossible to determine the will of the people. This helps to explain a paradoxical maxim formulated by Rousseau: "If, when an adequately informed people deliberates, the Citizens were to have no communication among themselves, the general will would always result from the large number of small differences, and the deliberation would always be good."[2] How very contradictory it seems to us today to conceive of information without communication!

For many political scientists, it is an article of faith that the practice of polling has made democracy scientific; some of them even dream of a computerized democracy operating in real time, in which the perpetual canvassing of opinion would make the state of the general will known at every instant. But the undecidability produced by the recursive loop of polling on itself, and, ultimately, on the act of voting, strongly suggests that this techno-optimism is misplaced.

Let us come back for a moment to the prophets of the Bible. These were extraordinary men who stood out from the crowd and made a strong impression on their neighbors. Their prophecies affected the world around them and the course of events for these purely human and social reasons; but also because those who heard them believed that the word of the prophet was the word of the Lord and that this word, which could not be heard directly but came to the prophet from on high, had the power to bring about the very thing that it announced.[3] We would say today that the word of the prophet had a *performative* power: by saying things, he brought them into being. Mind you, the prophet was well aware of this. One might be tempted to conclude that the prophet had the power to which political revolutionaries aspire: he spoke so that things would change in the direction that he wished. But this would be to overlook the fatalistic aspect of prophecy, which tells all things that will come to pass just as they are written down on the great scroll of history, immutably, ineluctably. This fatalism is apparent in Jeremiah (13:23): "Can the Ethiopian change his skin or the leopard his spots?"

Revolutionary prophecy, particularly in the form it came to acquire in Marxist doctrine, has preserved the highly paradoxical mixture of fatalism and human volition that characterizes biblical prophecy. Hans Jonas's observations on Marxism confirm that his metaphysical point of departure is the same as ours: "Here we have world-historical prognosis on a rational basis— and at the same time, through the unique equation of what must be with what ought to be, a goal-setting for the political *will*, which is thereby itself made a factor in proving the theory true after the latter's pre-affirmed truth had first motivated the will on its part. For the political action thus determined, which makes happen what must happen, this closed circuit creates a most peculiar mixture of colossal responsibility for the future with deterministic release from responsibility."[4]

Most biblical prophets knew very well how to find the solution to this equation, following the same strategy as Herbert Simon in the case of voting: they sought the *fixed point* of the problem, the point where human volition achieves the very thing that fate dictates. Biblical prophecy includes itself in its own discourse, one might say, for it sees itself as bringing about the very event that it announces as destiny. Its self-referentiality, in other words, is conscious. When a prophet foretells a catastrophe, he does not present the punishment it embodies as a threat, but as the eschatological fulfillment of a history that contains, as one of its decisive elements, the prophecy itself— including, in some cases, the fact that it produced no repentance, no change in the behavior of those who heard it. The case of Amos, a contemporary of Jonah, is particularly remarkable. Almost all the words of his prophecy are words of judgment and censure. And yet little by little, what began as a grim forecast of ruin and calamity is transformed into a prophecy of hope that points in the direction of a more merciful destiny—as if Amos's prophecy was aware of its own salvational effect. The case of Jonah is much more difficult, and for this reason we were destined to grapple with it. Jonah is faced with a problem that has no fixed point: no matter what the content of his prophesy, it will not be fulfilled. If he prophesies the repentance and conversion of the people of Nineveh, this will not happen. If he prophesies their destruction, he knows that this will not happen either. To be sure, he is not the one who determines the content of the prophecy, for he is only a spokesman; but the divine author of his prophecy would appear equally unable to escape this double bind.

Almost three thousand years later, Hans Jonas finds himself in the same predicament—he wishes to prophesy a catastrophe that he hopes will not occur, *so that* it will not occur. In other words, he can succeed in the ethical sphere only by failing in the metaphysical sphere. His problem—and ours— seems to have no fixed point. I maintain, however, that such a point can be found.

Jonas's dilemma is by far the most intractable of its kind. Rather than attack it directly, I should like to come back for a moment to the general case of prophets who manage to bring about the convergence, at some point in the future that they take as their endpoint, of two things: the causal sequence of events, of which the prophecy's own impact is a part, and the unfolding of an implacable destiny. The reader will recall that we encountered a like configuration earlier, in connection with von Foerster's theorem, except that there it had to do with mathematics; and also in connection with the autonomy of technology, except that there it had to do with economics. We must now take up the question afresh, bringing to bear the analytical tools of metaphysics—and keeping in mind that metaphysics is a rational discipline.

From sociological theory, and later economic theory, we have long been familiar with the notion of a self-fulfilling prophecy: a representation concerning the future that takes on the trappings of truth, not because it was true from the first, but because it triggers in those who share it a joint reaction that makes it if not true, then at least congruent with future reality. A forecast of the rate of increase in prices, for example, may be self-fulfilling if a sufficient number of individuals and firms adopt it as the basis for economic calculation. One might be tempted to say that the paradox I am trying to elucidate is just another self-fulfilling prophecy. But that would be to miss a crucial element of the reflexivity that obtains in this case: the prophet I am describing is aware of everything that I have just said when he fine-tunes the content of his prophecy. He anticipates the future *in the full knowledge* that it will come about in accordance with the logic of self-fulfilling prophecy. That logic can be readily described within the framework of traditional metaphysics.[5] But the additional degree of reflexivity introduced by the prophet's clear-sightedness about the status of the future that he foretells plunges us into an entirely different metaphysics—one that, I will now show, is precisely the metaphysics we have been seeking.

Is it possible to believe both that the future we foresee is the result of fate, and, at the same time, that we act causally upon that future by the very fact of predicting it and making our prediction public?[6] In fact, there is no metaphysical obstacle that prevents a person from simultaneously holding these two beliefs. To use David K. Lewis's terminology, it is a matter of believing: 1) that the future causally depends, at least in part, on what we do; and 2) that the future is counterfactually independent of what we do.

If it is possible for these two beliefs to coexist without contradiction, then that drives a wedge between causal and counterfactual dependence. It is true that there is a natural temptation to think of these two dependencies as being equivalent, in which case each would imply the other. The assumption that this is so I shall call "causalism." The traditional metaphysics of time, in the description of it given by Lewis that we examined in the last chapter, rests on causalism. We hold that our present actions cannot have a causal effect on the past, and we infer from this that the past is counterfactually independent of the present. We also hold that our present actions can have a causal effect on the future, and we infer from this that the future depends counterfactually on the present. From now on, following Lewis, I shall most often replace the cumbersome expressions "counterfactually independent of" and "counterfactually dependent on" by "fixed" and "open," respectively. In traditional metaphysics, the past is regarded as fixed and the future as open. This fixity and openness, it must be emphasized, hold with respect to a counterfactual power but not necessarily with respect to a causal power.

A fixed past and an open future: that is the way we "spontaneously" think of time—although not, as we shall see, in all circumstances. The *form* that corresponds to this spontaneous conception is familiar to all students of strategic behavior. It is that of a tree—a "decision tree," as it is called.

In this diagram, the possibilities preexist the moment when time chooses one of them, and they survive beyond this moment. But such moments occur at every point of the trajectory described by time's infinite arborescence. They are like the steps that each of us takes in the course of our life, from the

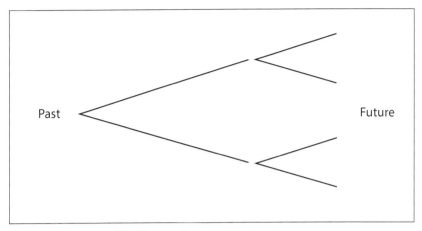

Time as a garden of forking paths, or occurring time

day of our birth to that of our death, and that trace, in Jorge Luis Borges's words, an "inconceivable figure."[7] In a memorable phrase quoted by Lewis, Borges dubbed this type of time a "garden of forking paths."[8] This "web of timelines that converge, fork, intersect or never meet for centuries, encompasses *all* possibilities," explains one of the protagonists of the detective story that bears this title. "Time forks, perpetually, into countless futures. In one of them, I am your enemy."[9]

Let us return now to the situation of the prophet as I have described it. In assuming that the future is fixed while also believing that he is the cause of it, at least in part, the prophet violates the principle of causalism. Is there anything wrong with this, from the metaphysical point of view?

Not necessarily. That there may be counterfactual dependence even in the absence of causal dependence is attested by many examples that can be constructed in a coherent manner. Here is one possible example. Imagine that somewhere today there is a man who missed his flight to New York from Boston on the morning of September 11, 2001. As a psychological matter, it is not implausible to suppose that he still shudders at the thought of this happenstance, and that it will continue to make him shudder as long as he lives. Why? Because he says to himself, 'If I hadn't missed my plane, I would have died in the horrific circumstances that the whole world witnessed.' What underlies this reasoning is, of course, the causalist hypothesis: 'Whether or not I missed my flight could not have any causal effect on the unfolding of the tragedy, and therefore no counterfactual effect; accordingly, if I had not missed the flight, the tragedy would have occurred in exactly the same way and I would have been counted among the victims.' But this inference is unwarranted, and any number of more or less plausible scenarios may be imagined in which it would be false.

Say, for example, that I was delayed by an accident on the highway leading to the airport. Suppose furthermore that one of the vehicles involved in the accident carried a government agent who had learned of the terrorists' plans and was rushing to the airport to thwart them. 'If the accident had not occurred, not only would I not have missed my plane but the catastrophe would have been avoided.' The relative implausibility of this scenario from a logistical standpoint must not be allowed to obscure the so-called "common-cause" schema that it is meant to illustrate: the occurrence of the accident is the cause of two events that are causally independent of each other, my delay and the failure to foil the terrorist plot. Such a schema justifies regarding two causally independent variables as counterfactually linked.

The configuration that is of greatest interest to us, however, arises where causal *dependence* is combined with counterfactual *independence*. Establishing the consistency of this relationship is much trickier.[10] One instance in particular comes to mind that will allow us to tie up several loose ends in the discussion up to this point. The theorists of "pure" competition posit that economic agents, producers, and consumers alike, take prices to be given, or fixed, which is to say independent of their actions.[11] These actions taken together make up the overall supply and demand for goods in the economy. The encounter of supply and demand in the marketplace is used in turn to explain the formation of prices. Very early on, Marxist economists objected to the utter incoherence, as it seemed to them, of crediting agents with a causal power over the formation of prices while at the same time holding that these same agents, oblivious to their power, should consider as given and fixed the results of their own actions. For Marxists, such a "contradiction" could be understood only as a reflection of the alienation endemic to capitalist society. Market theorists, for their part, saw no contradiction in what, as far as they were concerned, was merely the result of the search for a fixed point.

In truth, the hypothesis that economic agents take prices to be fixed is not contradictory, but neither is it as unremarkable as economists might like us to believe. As is now generally recognized, what economic theory, rational choice theory, and game theory call "equilibrium" has nothing to do with what this term originally meant in rational mechanics. Every decision problem involving two (or more) agents exhibits the phenomenon of *specularity*, meaning that each agent has to think about what the other thinks about what he himself thinks, and so on. A given type of equilibrium corresponds to a certain way of cutting off this potentially infinite regress at some point. By assuming prices to be fixed, market theory posits that the regress ends at the level of prices. But this theory has never really managed to provide a satisfactory foundation for what still today remains its key hypothesis. Economists generally content themselves with saying that the agents are too small for their actions to have an appreciable effect on prices. This claim—debatable in itself (consumers, for example, could join forces, form cooperatives or unions, and so on)—reveals above all that economists unhesitatingly adopt (without even knowing it) the causalist hypothesis. To justify the fixity of prices, they feel obliged to maintain that economic agents have only a minuscule *causal* power over prices—one that, at a first approximation, can therefore be neglected. The configuration that concerns us here never occurs to them. In reality, one should be able to assert without contradiction that agents have a causal power over prices and, at the same time, that they regard prices as *fixed*, not in the causal sense, but rather in the technical sense that I have given this term: prices are *counterfactually independent* of what the agents themselves do.

At this juncture it will be useful to recall von Foerster's theorem. It tells us that under certain precisely specified conditions, the situation of agents in a system that is beyond their power to control provides an objective basis for counterfactual conditional propositions of this sort: "If I had acted differently (for example, by increasing my demand for such-and-such a good), the overall price level would not have been affected by my decision." This, I maintain, is not in the least incompatible with the fact that agents have a causal power over prices and know it.

It may be objected that such agents are indeed "alienated" in the Marxist sense of the term. This need not be true. Agents may choose to behave *as if* they were alienated. But why would they do such a thing? Because, once again, they can coordinate their actions only if they find a way to avoid being trapped in the potentially infinite regress to which they are otherwise relegated by their need to know what others know of what they know, and so on. To put a halt to the reflexive action of specularity, the agents consciously decide, as a matter of *convention*, to regard a certain set of variables as fixed (that is, counterfactually independent of their actions), although they know full well they have a causal power over them. Such a configuration is perfectly conceivable without contradiction. It is the basis for the concept of a "coordination convention" developed by an important new school of economic thought.[12]

This example alone suffices, I believe, to show that causal dependence can go hand in hand with counterfactual independence. It will serve as a springboard for coming back to the much more complex question of temporality. First, however, I should note that no market theorist has ever seen the least contradiction between assuming, on the one hand, that prices are fixed and, on the other, that agents are endowed with free will. On the contrary, it is precisely because agents are able to deliberate about their choices that the hypothesis of price fixity takes on its full meaning: whether an individual does this or that in no way alters the prices on which he bases his decision.

With regard to decision problems involving time, it is usually taken for granted that agents hold the past to be fixed.[13] That is, they hold the past to be counterfactually independent of their actions. In metaphysical reasoning, the fixity of the past has acquired the status of a principle. The future, by contrast, is assumed to be open. A fixed past and an open future jointly constitute the time I described earlier, the garden of forking paths. Less poetically, I have proposed calling this conception of temporality *occurring time*. That is the expression I shall use from here on.

In occurring time, agents coordinate their actions with one another thanks to a convention, or shared understanding, according to which the past is unchanging and unchangeable. Indeed, this way of looking at the world seems so natural to us that we do not even think of it as a convention. The fact that we are all agreed in regarding the past as being fixed is what allows us to make promises, undertake commitments, enter into contracts— all fundamental components of the social bond. If I have committed myself to reimbursing a loan that you made me, nothing in the future will be able to alter the fact that I am so committed. A past crime may perhaps one day be pardoned, but nothing can cause it not to have taken place. The habitual tendency of totalitarian regimes to rewrite history only serves to emphasize the falsity of the account that they substitute in its place.

I nevertheless contend that another seemingly self-evident conception of time, in which we coordinate our actions with reference to a future held to be fixed, is no less familiar. Our experience of this time is facilitated, encouraged, organized—even imposed upon us—by many of the institutions of modern society. We are constantly being told what the more or less near future holds in store: the state of traffic on the highway tomorrow, the result of elections next month, the rate of inflation and economic growth next year, the change in greenhouse-gas emissions over the coming years, and so on. Yet economic forecasters and the other prophets of our day know quite well, as we do ourselves, that we are the ones who make the very future they herald as if it were written in the stars. Despite what might be taken for a metaphysical impropriety, we do not resist such predictions (except occasionally in the voting booth). I will try to bring out the coherence of this way of coordinating our actions with respect to the future.

What we learned by looking at the case of the market economy may serve as a guide. To suppose that an individual agent considers the future to be fixed in no way implies that he is unaware that the future depends causally, at least in part, on what he does now. Nor does it imply that he is not free to act otherwise than he does. This last point is tricky and needs to be examined more closely. The agent who takes the future as fixed assumes it to be counterfactually independent of his action. In his reasoning, while holding the future constant, he is going to decide on a present course of action. Say he chooses from among some number of options the one that seems to him the best. Now suppose the agent sees clearly that this option will make it impossible for the future he has predicted to come about. Does this impossibility mean that the world, having been condemned to non-existence, will implode in the next instant? No, of course not. What it shows is that the agent is not free to forecast any future at all. It goes without saying that in occurring time this is also true, but there the constraint is of a different kind. Prediction, as we have seen, consists in using a model to simulate the causal succession of phenomena that are indifferent to whether they are predicted or not. Recall in this connection the ethical dilemma that Hans Jonas identifies in our present situation: we have a moral obligation to forecast the remote consequences of our decisions, but those consequences are unforeseeable. In the case where the future, rather than the past, is assumed to be fixed, our ability to anticipate the future is constrained by the fact that the reaction to the anticipated

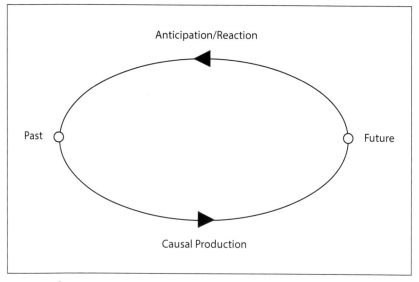

Projected time

future causally feeds back into the process of anticipation. Whereas occurring time has the form of a tree, the time that I am now describing has the form of a loop in which past and future mutually determine each other.

This other temporality is what I have dubbed projected time. It displays singular properties that are sometimes paradoxical, but no more so than Bergson's metaphysics, with which it has certain features in common. The principal one is this: since the future is assumed to be fixed, every event that belongs neither to the present nor to the future is an impossible event. Let us pause for a moment to consider what such a state of affairs involves.

One of the high points in the history of metaphysics came near its beginning. At about the time of Aristotle, a Greek philosopher named Diodorus Cronus formulated an aporia, or type of paradox, known as the Master Argument. Having laid down certain principles concerning the conditions of a free act, each of which is presented as being in agreement with common sense, indeed as having axiomatic force, Diodorus proceeds to demonstrate that they are mutually incompatible. The problem is therefore to decide which one (or more) of the axioms must be abandoned. The third axiom states: "There are possibilities which are not now and never will be realized."[14] It is plain that occurring time satisfies this principle and that projected time contradicts it. In projected time, it is the negation of the principle that is true: every possibility is realized, either in the present or in the future.

This point is crucial for our purposes here. In projected time, prudence can never take the form of prevention. Prevention presupposes that an undesirable event that is prevented is a possibility that is not realized. The event must be possible for us to have a reason to act; but if our action is effective, the event does not occur. The undesirable possibility, although it is not realized, must nevertheless retain a sort of reality—the same reality that is shared by all those possibilities that do not form a part of our actual world. This is what is meant by Clausewitz's famous aphorism in *On War*: "Possible engagements are to be regarded as real ones because of their consequences."[15] No such thing is conceivable in projected time, however. If prudence is conceivable in projected time at all, we know already that it cannot take the form of prevention.

"The memory of the future"—of the future as it is, not as it might be: this fine phrase is intelligible in projected time and projected time alone. In the foregoing diagram of the feedback loop, it is the upper arrow that carries the signals coming from the future described by Hans Jonas. This arrow reflects the activity of predicting. But beware! This is not the sort of prediction that is familiar to us from occurring time, which is modeled on the causal chain of physical phenomena. It is prediction that is conscious of its own effect on the future, that predicts the future as if it were fixed and at the same time caused, at least in part, by the effects of the prediction.

Projected time is not fatalist even though it postulates a fixed future. What makes projected time different from fatalism is that it is only too aware of the capacity of causal chains to *mimic* fatalism. In producing the impression of destiny, it seeks moreover to exploit this effect. Let us come back to the meaning of freedom in projected time. Once the loop has closed on its fixed point, which is the state of the future, anything that belongs neither to the past nor the future is impossible. There is nothing outside the actual world and the temporal trajectory that constitutes it. Everything in it is necessary. Freedom can be situated only in the mental activity of the person (or persons) who searches for the loop's fixed point "before" it is found. The future is then "still" unknown, an x in the sense of a mathematical unknown: even though it is unknown, one can perform all sorts of operations on it *as if* it were known, and thus determine its value. Freedom here is the ability to think of any future as given and to draw conclusions from it about the past that both anticipates that future and reacts to what is given. It is in this sense that one may say that *before* the future is determined, it is *not yet* necessary. But this "before" and this "not yet" are situated outside projected time. In projected time, the *simultaneous* determination of the past and future deprive these expressions of meaning.

Projected time is therefore a metaphysical fiction, albeit one that is both consistent and, as I shall go on to show, rational. But occurring time, "our" time, is no less a fiction. In metaphysics, one can do nothing more than construct such fictions. And yet they are indispensable to us, for they help us to think of ourselves as free in a world governed by causal determinism.

Aristotle, Leibniz, and Kant all constructed splendid fictions about occurring time. Christine Korsgaard, a student of Rawls and a leading Kantian philosopher in her own right, summarizes the point of these fictions in this way: "In order to do anything, you must simply ignore the fact that you are programmed, and decide what to do—just as if you were free."[16] Our ability to act coincides exactly with the extent to which we endow ourselves with the capacity to set in motion, by an effect of our will, new causal chains of events. To act as though we were free leads us to consider counterfactual conditionals of the type: "If I were to act otherwise than I am acting now, then such-and-such a thing would happen as a result."

The fiction that I have constructed under the name of projected time[17] brings together ideas found in a number of earlier philosophers, although it does not appear as a coherent whole in any of them. One thinks of Spinoza, for whom to be free is to acquiesce in necessity; of Bergson, of course, for whom the sudden appearance of something radically new modifies the truth value of modal propositions concerning the past; of Heidegger's notion of resoluteness (*Entschlossenheit*), and of the paradoxical ability to "choose one's fate" that it entails; of Nietzsche, who spoke of the "memory of will"; finally, of Sartre and his formula: "To be finite ... is to choose oneself, which is to say to announce to oneself that which one is, by projecting oneself toward one possible rather than any other."[18]

In the fiction of projected time, I consider myself as being determined by an essence, to use Sartre's vocabulary, but the essence is unknown. I am not free, in any possible world, to act contrary to this essence. How, then, can I believe in the fiction of my freedom? By acting *as if* I were free to choose this essence by choosing my existence (in this way expressions such as "choosing one's fate" and "determining oneself" become meaningful). The counterfactual conditionals that I will use in my practical reasoning will here be of the backtracking type: "If I did this rather than that, my essence would *have had to be* this one rather than that one for such a thing to have happened as a result."[19]

If we transpose to the temporal domain our analysis of the hypothesis of fixed prices in the theory of the market, we can draw the following lesson. The very alienation of agents—the fact that they treat the future as an inflexible destiny rather than seeing it as the consequence of their own actions—facilitates and encourages the coordination of their actions with respect to a future regarded as fixed. If it can also be shown that this mode of coordination sometimes has desirable properties, or at least ones less undesirable than other conventions, then it would follow that a future rigidified into fate is at once a poison and a remedy. This, I maintain, is exactly our situation today in the face of new threats.

It is obvious that one may—and occasionally must—situate oneself in projected time without any alienation. This is what happens when a collective undertaking galvanizes a group of people or an entire nation around a desirable common *project*. The best example that I know is that of state economic planning in France as conceived by Pierre Massé and brilliantly summed up by Roger Guesnerie. Planning, Guesnerie said, "aimed at obtaining by means of consultation and study an image of the future that is sufficiently optimistic to be desirable and sufficiently credible to give rise to the actions that will bring about its own realization."[20] Plainly this statement makes sense only within the metaphysics of projected time, whose loop linking past and future it perfectly describes. Coordination is achieved on the basis of an *image* of the future that is capable of closing the loop between a causal production of the future and the self-fulfilling expectation of it.

The premises are now in place for the paradoxical formulation of a doomsaying solution to the problem of the threats looming over our future. It is a matter of achieving coordination on the basis of a negative project that takes the form of a fixed future *that one does not want*. One might think of recasting Guesnerie's formula to speak of obtaining, by means of scientific modeling and reflection on human purpose, "an image of the future that is sufficiently catastrophic to be repellent and sufficiently credible to give rise to the actions that will keep it from being realized." But this way of putting the matter leaves an essential point unresolved. An undertaking of this nature would seem to be tarnished by a disabling logical defect: self-contradiction. For if the undesirable future is avoided—if it never comes into existence—how can it have provided the basis for our coordination? The impasse remains complete.

CHAPTER 12

The Rationality of Doomsaying

If we are compelled to think here first of the destiny of the natural world as this world has been conditioned by mankind, *a destiny that stares at us from the future*, it turns out that the appropriate sentiment is a mixture of fear and guilt: fear, because prediction correctly shows us terrible *realities*; guilt, because we are conscious of our own role in their unfolding.

—Hans Jonas, *Pour une éthique du futur*

This is the way the world ends
Not with a bang but a whimper.

—T. S. Eliot, *The Hollow Men*

f Hans Jonas poses as a prophet of doom, if he announces *urbi et orbi* the catastrophe to come, it is because he has in mind, not the Biblical prophets, but instead the Cassandras, Laocoöns, and other prophets of antiquity whose special misfortune was that their warnings were fated never to be heeded.[1] Jonas repeatedly laments that we do not grant sufficient weight to the future reality of catastrophe. The prospect of disasters to come makes

131

no impression on us, either intellectually or emotionally. "The imagined fate of future men," Jonas remarks, "let alone that of the planet, which affects neither me nor anyone else still connected with me by the bonds of love or just of coexistence, does not of itself have this influence upon our feeling. *And yet it 'ought' to have it—that is*, we *should allow it this influence . . ."*[2] The "emotional aspect of the morally required vision of the future" is for him no less important than the cognitive dimension. "The *factual* knowledge of futurology," Jonas emphasizes, "[must] awaken in us a *feeling* that encourages us to act in a way that satisfies our [moral] responsibility."[3]

In every aspect of Jonas's ontology, which I have not taken up here, one meets with the same plea. Thus, for example, the difficulty in asserting the moral rights of generations yet unborn is that "only that *has* a claim [that] *makes* claims—for which it must first of all *exist*. . . . The non-existent makes no demands and can therefore not suffer violation of its rights. . . . Above all, it has no right to exist at all before it in fact exists. The claim to existence begins only with existence. But the ethic we seek is concerned with just this *not-yet-existent*."[4] The challenge facing us is therefore always bound up with the lack of being peculiar to representations of misfortune. This was already the case in Ivan Illich's critique of modern industrial society, where the evil is invisible, hidden within the detours of work and heteronomy. Our duty, then, is to flush it out from its hiding place.

Nietzsche held that nature, in bringing forth mankind, set itself the "paradoxical task" of breeding an "animal *with the right to make promises*." Humanity thus learned "to see and anticipate distant eventualities as if they belonged to the present."[5] I have tried to show that only the metaphysics of projected time can account for this *actualization of the future*: by putting past and future face to face with each other, it makes them twins. In occurring time, successful prevention converts catastrophe into an unrealized possibility, a sort of ontological phantom whose weight of reality is not great enough to sustain the will to keep it out of the actual world. The self-refuting character of successful prevention is not a matter of logic since in this case it involves representation and will. Projected time, on the other hand, firmly inscribes catastrophe in the reality of the future, so much so that a successful prevention cannot help nullifying itself—only this time for a logical reason: since there is no place for catastrophe in the empty set of unactualized possibilities, it disappears into non-being. This logical impasse, in exactly the terms I have just used to describe it, lies at the heart of the debate about the morality and efficacy of nuclear deterrence. As it happens, this same debate shows us a way out.

It is not because the precautionary principle has its source, as some contend, in the historiography of the Cold War that I now turn to the topic of nuclear deterrence. I do so solely because it allows us to see that our metaphysical conundrum admits of a solution. It is hardly accidental that David K. Lewis counts among the American philosophers who actively participated in the critical reflections on the logic of the infamous "balance of terror." That is the crucible in which Lewis refined some of his most important concepts.[6] I may add that if there is any domain where a "heuristics of fear" has had an essential role, it is unquestionably nuclear warfare, which has placed the most sophisticated tools of rational thought in the service of the most extreme madness.

I obviously have in mind the "logic" of MAD—mutually assured destruction (or, more accurately, mutual vulnerability). The basic schema is very simple: each nation offers up its own population to a possible holocaust through retaliation by the other. Under these circumstances, security becomes the daughter of terror. If either nation took steps to protect itself, the other might believe that its adversary believes itself to be invulnerable, and so, in order to prevent a first strike, might strike first itself. In a nuclear regime, nations appear at once vulnerable and invulnerable: vulnerable because they can perish from attack by an adversary; invulnerable because they will not perish before bringing about their attacker's demise—something they will always be capable of doing, no matter how powerful the strike that reduces them to rubble. Nuclear deterrence doubtless contributed to that paradoxical peace known as the Cold War. Yet one may still wonder whether it was not—and whether it does not remain today—a moral monstrosity. Such scruples are habitually dismissed as relics of the past, completely obsolete. The American anti-missile shield will, we are told, transport us into an entirely different world, less unfamiliar no doubt than the one that the tragedy of September 11, 2001, abruptly ushered in. In reality, the world promised by *Star Wars* is, I believe, infinitely more dangerous than that of the Cold War. But this is not the place to discuss that subject.[7] Let me stress once again that I am interested here only in the metaphysical foundations of the debate about nuclear deterrence. But I must note one more point. The indispensable condition of a balance of terror is that the adversaries exhibit that minimal degree of rationality that consists in wishing to stay alive. The doomsaying position that I am trying to elaborate itself appeals to the wisdom and rationality of human beings—a rationality that goes far beyond a mere desire for self-preservation. If it were to turn out that these assumptions are invalid, there would be nothing left to do but despair of humanity's ineradicable folly.

"Our submarines will be capable of killing fifty million people in half an hour," a French strategist once blithely observed. "We think that this suffices to deter any adversary."[8] The incomparably horrifying threat that such a statement expresses is the very essence of deterrence. Many people will agree that killing fifty million innocent persons[9] is an incommensurable evil, even if it is done in retaliation for an immensely damaging first strike. By itself alone, would not the *intention* to commit such an act be no less colossal an evil? If I conceive a plan to kill you, and an unforeseen event prevents me from going through with it, one may wonder whether I am morally any less culpable than if I had been able to carry out my plan successfully.

Does moral philosophy enable us to respond to such questions? The answer will not be found in France. French philosophers and military officers do not talk to each other, and so, by default, it has fallen to politicians to decide one of the most fundamental questions for the life of the nation. Once again we find democracy being used as an excuse for evading the duty of moral reflection—as if the ritual of voting could ever replace rational debate. We must look instead to America for guidance in this matter.

The principal argument advanced in support of deterrence is easily grasped. Deterrence is said to be the only way to prevent a conflict from being unleashed whose escalation would lead to a cataclysm on both sides. Whether or not this was actually true during the Cold War is beside the point. We have forever lost our innocence, in the sense that nobody can now rule out the return of a MAD structure where it would be true. The refusal to form the intention to kill tens of millions of people would then be causally sufficient to produce tens of millions of murders, not only on one's own side but on the other's as well. When the gap between the consequences of two actions is exceedingly great—in this case, between the survival of humanity and its possible self-annihilation—it would be irresponsible not to adopt a consequentialist criterion, which under the foregoing hypotheses leads to the following conclusion:

The Rationality of Doomsaying 135

1. It is right to form the intention to do p, where "do p" stands for "cause the death of tens of millions of innocents." And yet intuitively we feel no less sure that:

2. It is wrong to do p. These two assumptions land us in a contradiction if they are supplemented by the following principle, which articulates an idea that is very deeply rooted in our traditional ethics:

3. It is wrong to form the intention to do x if it is wrong to do x.

This, according to the philosopher Gregory Kavka, is the paradox into which we are inescapably thrust by the mere possibility of a MAD structure.[10] Never before in the history of human affairs has the conflict between common-sense morality, expressed by (3), and consequentialist rationality, which yields (1), been so agonizing. The advocates of deterrence argue that (1) is irrefutable, and their critics say the same of (3). It is hard to avoid the suspicion that each captures only a part of the truth.

Some of those who endorse (3) have been reduced to defending the awkward position that it is always true except in the case of nuclear deterrence. Alternatively, it might be emphasized that the intention to do p is merely conditional, but this does not succeed in removing the fundamental difficulty. If I form a plan to kill you when certain conditions that are beyond my control have been satisfied, the moral status of my intention is the same as if it were unconditional. To this it may be objected that a deterrent intention is not a conditional intention in the usual sense of the term. The conditions that would lead me to do p are so little out of my control that what I hope to achieve by forming the intention to do p is precisely to ensure that these conditions will not be satisfied. The French nuclear strike force does not exist in order to wipe out fifty million innocents; it exists in order to prevent from being satisfied the conditions that would lead us to wipe out fifty million innocents. The deterrent intention could thus be considered "self-refuting" or "self-invalidating."

Is this argument enough to ease the anxieties of those who fear a nuclear apocalypse? Suppose for a moment that it is, and that we are sure our leaders will never be placed in circumstances that would persuade them to push the nuclear button. But in that case our deterrent capability would appear to lose all efficacy. For deterrence to work, one must not rule out the *possibility* of the worst coming to pass, even if one rules out its actual occurrence. And the simple fact of making the worst possible is an evil in itself—at least that is what the adversaries of deterrence will assert.

We can clarify the dilemma using the conceptual tools at our disposal. For deterrence to be both effective and morally defensible, the thing used as a threat, namely, nuclear apocalypse, must be an event that is a possibility, but one that is unrealized. The event must be a possibility so that, even unrealized, it may have an impact on the real world. But obviously it must remain unrealized if we want to avoid the ultimate catastrophe. Note that these are simply necessary conditions. The logical structure of deterrence is identical to what we already saw in the case of prevention. Whether we are talking about nuclear war or the catastrophes hovering over humanity's economic and industrial development, the main obstacle to effective prevention or deterrence is that we do not believe in the reality of the unrealized possibility. The danger is not credible.

The better part of the strategic and technical literature on nuclear deterrence is concerned with the lack of credibility of the threat on which it is supposed to rest. I will not summarize these debates here because only the logical structure of the problem is relevant for my argument. It goes without saying that the reasons for the non-credibility of the nuclear threat are not of the same nature as the ones that I have already examined at length in the context of economic or industrial development. In the first case, the nuclear threat is made by an agent (even if it is a collective agent such as a state) and results from a deliberate intention; in the second, calamity swoops down on its victims as if it had come out of nowhere, *like an act of fate*. Now, so long as the agent who threatens a lethal and suicidal nuclear escalation if his demands are not met is minimally rational, we can be sure that when push comes to shove—say, after a first strike has destroyed part of his territory—he will not carry out his threat. The very premise of MAD is that mutual destruction is assured if either party upsets the balance of terror. What statesman, having in the aftermath of a first strike only remnants of a devastated nation left to defend, would run the risk, by launching a vengeful second strike, of putting an end to the human race? In a world of sovereign states exhibiting this minimal degree of rationality, the nuclear threat has no credibility whatsoever.

At this stage the debate over deterrence is at exactly the same point where we had arrived when we discovered that it is not uncertainty, scientific

The Rationality of Doomsaying

or otherwise, that necessitates a strategy different from traditional prevention, but rather the future catastrophe's lack of credibility.

The next step in the argument is crucial. It was taken when the shrewdest defenders of the strategy of mutual vulnerability realized that the concept of a deterrent *intention* had to be jettisoned altogether. We have just seen that this concept had always been hobbled by the risk of self-refutation. The turning point in the debate came with the revolutionary idea that the threat confronting the enemy had to be presented not as an intentional act, but as a fatality, an accident. According to the new doctrine, the mere *existence* of nuclear arsenals that create a structure of mutual vulnerability suffices to make both parties infinitely cautious, independently of any intention or reason to act. After all, no one in their right mind would taunt a tiger while the door of its cage is unlocked.[11] If one may still speak of rationality here, it is, as the philosopher Steven Lee puts it, "the kind of rationality in which the agent contemplates the abyss and simply decides never to get too close to the edge."[12] The accidental triggering of a process of escalation that spins out of control thus became an integral part of deterrence. The importance of this development for our purposes here can scarcely be overstated. With this doctrine of "existential deterrence," whatever distance had separated the nuclear threat from the catastrophes associated with industrial development vanishes altogether. In both cases, evil now assumes the form of a fatality.

In the United States, the military strategist Bernard Brodie was one of the most perceptive advocates of the new doctrine. "It is the curious paradox of our time," Brodie observed in the early 1970s, "that one of the foremost factors making [nuclear] deterrence really work and work well is the lurking fear that in some massive confrontation crisis it might fail. Under these circumstances *one does not tempt fate*. If we were absolutely certain that nuclear deterrence would be 100 per cent effective against nuclear attack, then it would cease to have much if any deterrent value against non-nuclear wars."[13]

A cursory reading may give the impression that Brodie's explanation is easily grasped: perfect deterrence is self-refuting, whereas imperfect deterrence can be effective. I contend, however, that neither of these theses can be demonstrated (or even expressed in a way that makes sense) within the traditional framework of practical reason, which is to say in terms of beliefs, desires, intentions, and decisions: in short, in terms of strategy. Brodie's dual thesis requires another metaphysics, another conception of time—what I call projected time.

Let us begin with the thesis that perfect deterrence is self-refuting. In occurring time, the time in which strategists operate, it can be asserted only at the price of committing a cardinal metaphysical fallacy, namely, that of inferring impossibility from non-actuality. This is exactly the error into which defenders of nuclear deterrence fall when, in response to the charge that they have made the unacceptable possible, they move surreptitiously from saying "I will never press the button" to "It is impossible that I press the button." In occurring time, if deterrence works perfectly, the threat of apocalypse becomes an unrealized possibility, and this possibility continues to exert its deterrent effect on the actual world. If it does not work, it will not in the least be because the threat refutes itself, but because, as a mere possibility waved about like a red flag, it is not credible. The logical error that manifests itself in occurring time amounts to confusing the two main arguments advanced over the years by the critics of nuclear deterrence: the lack of credibility of the threat, on the one hand, and the self-refuting character of successful deterrence, on the other. These two arguments rest on entirely different metaphysical foundations.

In projected time, by contrast, the move from non-actuality to impossibility, far from being a fallacy, is one of the basic properties of the underlying metaphysics: anything that does not exist, either now or in the future, is impossible. It is therefore true in projected time that every successful act of deterrence or prevention—by the very fact that it succeeds, and thereby relegates to non-existence the realization of the threat—nullifies itself. Every preventive measure that succeeds appears for this very reason to be useless, having been undertaken in order to banish from the world a nonexistent evil.[14] What in occurring time would appear to be a blatant sophism becomes a valid inference in projected time.

This conclusion lands us back in the same impasse at which we arrived before. We had wanted to provide a basis for doomsaying in the metaphysics of projected time, the idea being to achieve coordination by taking as fixed an undesirable future. This negative project, or anti-project—concentrating attention on a catastrophic future so that it will not occur—appeared to us as necessarily contradictory, since, if it succeeds, the future on which we concentrate will turn out not to have been the future at all, but an impossible event.

The Rationality of Doomsaying

I now come to the second of the two theses advanced by Bernard Brodie, namely, that uncertainty regarding the effectiveness of deterrence is what makes it effective. This is the thesis that freed the deterrence doctrine from the impasse in which it was stuck, wedged between non-credibility and self-invalidation. Uncertainty, accident or chance pointed to a way out by reestablishing both the credibility and stability of the nuclear threat and thus restoring its deterrent power. Everything hinges, as we shall presently see, on the metaphysical status of this uncertainty.

The idea of treating chance and uncertainty as a *strategic* solution to the general problem of deterrence was not new. Made famous by game theorist Thomas Schelling,[15] it has to some extent withstood the test of time. The idea was that it may sometimes be *rational to mimic irrationality*, in order to leave one's adversary in doubt about one's true intentions.[16] Given repeated confrontations, the antagonists may thereby acquire the reputation of being reckless thugs who will stop at nothing to get what they want, and each of them, even if he suspects the other of bluffing, but bluffing with good reason, will find it rational to yield. In this way a threat might become credible, and thereby have a deterrent effect. The undeniable fascination of mirror games of this sort is apt, however, to obscure the fact that they lose all point in situations of mutual vulnerability. In this case, by construction, the game is played only once—and that is one time too many.

Uncertainty of the strategic kind is clearly not the solution that Brodie had in mind. Faced with the unthinkable—having to carry out his threat in the event that deterrence fails—no rational player in a MAD game would leave the world's fate to a lottery or a round of Russian roulette: he would yield and refrain from retaliating. Strategic uncertainty naturally belongs to the metaphysics of occurring time. Our only remaining option at this stage of our journey is to rethink the meaning of uncertainty within the framework of projected time.

For deterrence that relies on uncertainty to be truly effective, one must renounce strategy once and for all and decide not to decide. But this way of stating the matter is not sufficiently precise. It could be interpreted along the lines of the "Doomsday Machine" dreamed up one day by a sightly daft nuclear strategist and brought to the screen by Stanley Kubrick in his surreal film *Dr. Strangelove* (1964). The underlying principle, also theorized by Schelling, is simple: by making retaliation automatic, one ties one's own hands.[17] But that would still be strategy. Brodie is careful to say something quite different, even if it obliges him to introduce an enigma that he leaves unexplained. Brody, too, invokes destiny or fatality. Not the conditional fatality that would be expressed by a proposition of the type: "If you attack me, it is inevitable that I will blow up everything." In that case one would still be in the realm of intentionality. The fatality in question here is both without conditions and improbable. *It is as if the apocalypse were written in the future, although the chance of its occurring is, mercifully, extremely small.* The solution consists in making a destiny of mutual annihilation: a highly risky game, but one that can be justified from the standpoint of prudence, since allowing deterrence to be only imperfectly effective is what keeps it from collapsing into self-refutation. These notions seem to add up to a meaningful whole, but they plainly have not hitherto been conceptualized in an adequate manner. I hold that the metaphysics of projected time makes it possible to give them the rigor they require. I must limit myself here to indicating the essential outlines of a demonstration that I have developed in greater technical detail elsewhere.[18]

Let us first consider things from a formal point of view. If we ask on what type of fixed point the loop that links the future to the past in projected time closes, it is clear that in the case at hand the catastrophic event itself cannot be that fixed point: the signals that it would send back toward the past (to borrow Jonas's memorable image once more) would trigger the actions that would keep the catastrophic future from being realized. This is why perfect deterrence is self-refuting. For signals from the future to reach the past without giving rise to the very thing that will abolish the source of those signals, there must subsist, inscribed in the future, an imperfection in the closure of the loop. Earlier I proposed recasting Roger Guesnerie's statement of what was once the ambition of French economic planners so that it could serve as the maxim of a rational form of doomsaying: one whose mission would be to obtain, by means of scientific modeling and reflection on human purpose, "an image of the future that is sufficiently catastrophic to be repellent and sufficiently credible to give rise to the actions that will keep it from being realized." I observed, however, that no sooner was this maxim uttered than it collapsed into self-refutation. Now we can see how to amend this formulation so as to save it from such an undesirable end. We need only add a few words, as follows: "an image of the future that is sufficiently catastrophic to be repellent and sufficiently credible to give rise to the actions that will keep it from being realized, *barring an accident.*"

One may wish to quantify the probability of this accident. Let us say that it is an epsilon, ε, by definition small or very small. The preceding explanation may then be expressed more succinctly: it is because there is a probability ε that deterrence will not work that it works with a probability $1-\varepsilon$. What might seem at first to be a tautology (as it obviously would be in the metaphysics of occurring time) is absolutely not one here, since the preceding proposition cannot be true for $\varepsilon = o$.[19] The fact that, as we have just seen, the probability that deterrence will not work must, in the case at hand, be strictly positive is what allows for the inscription of catastrophe in the future; moreover, it is by virtue of its inscription in the future that deterrence is effective, *with a margin of error* ε. Note, by the way, that it would be altogether incorrect to say that it is the *possibility* of an error, having a probability ε, that preserves the effectiveness of deterrence—as if the error and the absence of error constituted the two branches of a bifurcation. There are no forking paths in projected time. The error is not only possible; it is actual—written in time indelibly, like a slip of the pen.[20] In other words, the very thing that threatens us may be our only hope of salvation. This, I believe, is the most profound interpretation that can be given to what Hans Jonas called the heuristics of fear.

Humanity today is not playing a MAD game with adversaries called Nature, Technology, or Time. If, like Oedipus, it set out on a quest to find the culprit, it would end up coming face to face with itself. Behind the interceding natural and artificial barriers that keep men from falling upon one another in a murderous free-for-all, mankind never deals with anyone other than itself. This is a tale that has only one protagonist, even if the evil that threatens it assumes the form of fate. This fate is not an agent; it has no intentions. But the logical structure is exactly the same in the situation of mutually assured destruction. Beneath the surface appearance of twin antagonists inextricably bound together by their mimetic rivalry, one finds a single actor: humanity, grappling once more with its own violence, which assumes the form of an apocalyptic destiny. In both cases, the evil has no author; it is devoid of intention. The ruse in which we must place our hopes consists not in pretending that this evil does not exist, but in acting *as if* we were its victim—while keeping in mind that we are solely and uniquely the cause of what happens to us. This double game, this stratagem, is perhaps the necessary condition for our survival.

In projected time, time is ensnared in a loop that closes hermetically upon itself, as if past and future were forever tossing a ball back and forth between them. And yet, as in the case of biblical prophecy, this closure is simultaneously an opening. The temporal loop closes upon itself at the prophesied doom; but, like a supplement of life and hope, time continues beyond the point of closure. The opening arises from the fact that our fate has the status of an accident, of an error that it is within our power not to commit. From this moment on, we know that we are embarked on a voyage with a time-bomb on board. It is up to us alone to see to it that its explosion—inscribed as a highly improbable fatality—does not occur. We are condemned to permanent vigilance.

Our present understanding of the phenomenon of programmed cell death or cellular self-destruction has led the biologist Jean-Claude Ameisen to argue that the necessary condition of life is the perpetual suppression of suicide at the cellular level.[21] Life in its positive aspect must be conceived, he says, as the suppression of the suppression, the "negation of a negation," for it owes its existence to "the negation of a negative event—self-destruction."[22]

In much the same way, enlightened doomsaying urges us to regard the further existence of human society as resulting from the negation of an act of self-destruction—one engraved in a future that has been frozen into fate. In the hope, to paraphrase Borges, that this future, however inevitable it may be, nevertheless will not happen.

Notes

PROLOGUE. A TIME OF CATASTROPHES

1. Henri Bergson, *The Two Sources of Morality and Religion*, trans. R. Ashley Audra and Cloudesley Brereton, with the assistance of W. Horsfall Carter (Garden City, NY: Doubleday, 1935), 159–60. Bergson refers here to the feeling James experienced during the devastating San Francisco earthquake of April 1906. [English version slightly modified.—Trans.]

2. Ibid., 159. [English version slightly modified.—Trans.] The emphasis is mine.

3. Henri Bergson, "The Possible and the Real," in *The Creative Mind: An Introduction to Metaphysics*, trans. Mabelle L. Andison (New York: Philosophical Library, 1946), 121.

4. Ibid., 118–19. The emphasis in the first instance is Bergson's, in the second instance mine.

5. One may think here of the successful efforts to neutralize the Y2K bug and prevent a universal computer collapse in the year 2000. When the collapse did not take place, many critics deemed those efforts to have been a waste of resources.

CHAPTER 1. A SINGULAR POINT OF VIEW

1. Timothy O'Riordan and James Cameron, "The History and Contemporary Significance of the Precautionary Principle," in Timothy O'Riordan and James Cameron, eds., *Interpreting the Precautionary Principle* (London: Cameron May, 1994), 12.

143

2. The report commissioned by the French government on the precautionary principle goes so far as to describe this renunciation in the following terms: "In the absence of certainty, precaution consists in giving precedence to procedural rigor. When the 'truth' of a situation and the 'reality' of a risk cannot be established, it is the rigor of the procedures followed, and the meticulousness shown by those responsible for devising, executing, and monitoring them, that become the dominant values"; see Philippe Kourilsky and Geneviève Viney, eds., *Le principe de précaution: Rapport au Premier ministre* (Paris: Odile Jacob, 2000), 21.

I reject this claim, and join Hans Jonas in holding that "the *uncertainty* of all long-term projections . . . is in its turn to be taken as a fact, for the right treatment of which ethics has to find a principle *which itself is no longer an uncertain one*"; see *The Imperative of Responsibility: In Search of an Ethics for the Technological Age*, translated by the author in collaboration with David Herr (Chicago: University of Chicago Press, 1984), 34 [the emphasis at the end is mine]. Although my solution to the problem is not the same as Jonas's, I am no more resigned than he was to the vagaries of collective procedures. It is a cause for regret in my view that a scientist as distinguished as Philippe Kourilsky and a jurist as clear-sighted as Geneviève Viney should feel themselves obliged to put quotation marks around the words *truth* and *reality*, as if they were making a concession to "post-modern" thought.

3. Corinne Lepage and François Guery, *La politique de précaution* (Paris: Presses Universitaires de France, 2001), 198.

4. See Jean-Marie Domenach, *Le retour du tragique* (Paris: Seuil, 1967).

5. See Jean-Pierre Dupuy and Jean Robert, *La trahison de l'opulence* (Paris: Presses Universitaires de France, 1976).

6. See Ivan Illich, *Medical Nemesis: The Expropriation of Health* (New York: Pantheon, 1976).

7. See Jean-Pierre Dupuy, *On the Origins of Cognitive Science: The Mechanization of the Mind*, trans. M. B. DeBevoise (Cambridge, MA: The MIT Press, 2008); also *Les savants croient-ils en leurs théories? Une lecture philosophique de l'histoire des sciences cognitives* (Paris: Éditions de l'INRA, 2000).

8. Alexis de Tocqueville, *Democracy in America*, 2 vols., trans. Gerald Bevan (London: Penguin, 2003), 1.1.15, 14.

9. Hans Jonas, *Pour une éthique du futur*, trans. Sabine Cornille and Philippe Ivernel (Paris: Payot-Rivages, 1998), 104.

CHAPTER TWO. SACRIFICE, COUNTERPRODUCTIVITY, AND ETHICS, OR THE LOGIC OF THE DETOUR

1. See Jon Elster, *Leibniz et la formation de l'esprit capitaliste* (Paris: Aubier Montaigne, 1975); also *Ulysses and the Sirens: Studies in Rationality and Irrationality* (Cambridge: Cambridge University Press, 1979).

Notes   145

2. See especially Alain Renaut, *The Era of the Individual: A Contribution to a History of Subjectivity*, trans. M. B. DeBevoise and Franklin Philip (Princeton, NJ: Princeton University Press, 1997), 61–87.

3. Louis Dumont, *Essays on Individualism: Modern Ideology in Anthropological Perspective*, trans. Paul Hockings (Chicago: University of Chicago Press, 1986), 251.

4. See Jean-Pierre Dupuy, "De l'émancipation de l'économie: Retour sur 'Das Adam Smith Problem,'" *L'Année Sociologique* 37 (1987): 311–42. [An English version can be found in J.-P. Dupuy, "Invidious Sympathy in *The Theory of Moral Sentiments*," *The Adam Smith Review* 2 (2006): 96–121.—Trans.]

5. See Jean-Pierre Dupuy, "On the Rationality of Sacrifice," *Contagion: Journal of Violence, Mimesis, and Culture* 10, no. 1 (2003): 23–39.

6. I use this term in the sense that Louis Dumont gives it, without the least reference to a deliberate intent to obscure the truth of social relations or to any sort of "false consciousness." An ideology is the system of ideas and values that govern the imagination of a particular society.

7. Elster goes so far as to say that natural selection, in creating human beings—creatures that are capable of reasoning strategically and looking beyond local maxima—"has transcended itself"; see *Ulysses and the Sirens*, 16.

8. See the appendix ("À la recherche du temps gagné") that I contributed to the second French edition of Illich's work on transportation, *Énergie et Équité* (Paris: Seuil, 1975), 71–80.

9. In all of this I am afraid I did little more than translate Illich's argument into mathematical formulas. Whereas Illich stubbornly clung to religious language, I insisted no less obstinately on logic and mechanistic explanation. I explain my reasons for this in the introduction to my *Ordres et désordres: Enquête sur un nouveau paradigme* (Paris: Seuil, 1982), 11–28.

10. See Jean-Pierre Dupuy, "Le travail contreproductif," *Le Monde de l'économie* (15 October 1996). For the original calculations, see Dupuy, "À la recherche du temps gagné" (the appendix to Illich's *Énergie et Équité* cited in the note above).

11. An accurate comparison would require taking into account not the bicycle's actual average speed, but rather its generalized speed. Even so, since the cost of purchasing and maintaining a bicycle is relatively very small, the difference between the two figures is minimal.

12. The utilitarian variant of consequentialism takes the algebraic sum of pains and pleasures as the overall value to be maximized.

13. See Jean-Pierre Dupuy, "Éthique et rationalité," in Monique Canto-Sperber, ed., *Dictionnaire d'éthique et de philosophie morale* (Paris: Presses Universitaires de France, 1996), 1252–1258.

14. See Samuel Scheffler, *The Rejection of Consequentialism: A Philosophical Investigation of the Considerations Underlying Rival Moral Conceptions*, 2nd ed. (Oxford: Clarendon

Press, 1994), especially 35–36 and 70–79; also "Agent-Centred Restrictions, Rationality, and the Virtues," *Mind* 94 (1985): 409–19, reprinted in ibid., 133–51 and in Samuel Scheffler, ed., *Consequentialism and Its Critics* (Oxford: Oxford University Press, 1988), 243–60.

15. Robert Nozick, *Anarchy, State, and Utopia* (New York: Basic Books, 1974), 28–29.

16. This reversal is movingly depicted by Steven Spielberg in the film *Saving Private Ryan* (1998). At the outset Captain Miller looks at the world in a utilitarian—and therefore sacrificial—way, constantly weighing the lives lost by delivering men to slaughter against the much larger number ("ten times that many") that are thereby saved. He is sent on a mission to save one soldier, a lone, almost anonymous one (the American army was full of Ryans), for whose life he will give (not sacrifice) the lives of most of his men, and his own as well. The film admirably shows how this mission, which he and his men initially consider to be senseless, gradually comes to appear to them as the only thing that can give meaning to their experience of war.

17. See Michel Serres's fine meditation on this theme, "One God or a Trinity?" *Contagion: Journal of Violence, Mimesis, and Culture* 1 (1994): 1–17.

18. See Ulrich Beck, *Risk Society: Towards a New Modernity*, trans. Mark Ritter (London: Sage, 1992); also the essays collected in *World Risk Society* (Cambridge: Polity, 1999).

19. Peter L. Berger, *Pyramids of Sacrifice: Political Ethics and Social Change* (New York: Basic Books, 1975).

20. See Henri Hubert and Marcel Mauss, *Sacrifice: Its Nature and Function*, trans. W. D. Halls (Chicago: University of Chicago Press, 1964).

CHAPTER 3. FATE, RISK, AND RESPONSIBILITY

1. Jonas, *Pour une éthique du futur*, 105.

2. Ivan Illich, *Medical Nemesis* (New York: Pantheon Books, 1976), 261–62. Translation altered.

3. Ibid., 261.

4. Ibid., 263.

5. See René Dubos, *Man Adapting* (New Haven, CT: Yale University Press, 1965), 344–68.

6. These quotations are taken from "Évolution scientifique," the third in a series of pamphlets published by *Prospective et Santé Publique* under the general title *Recherche, Médicament, Prospective* (Paris, March 1971).

7. Ivan Illich, *Medical Nemesis* (New York: Pantheon Books, 1976), 92.

8. André Gorz [Michel Bosquet], *Ecology as Politics*, trans. Patsy Vigderman and Jonathan Cloud (Boston: South End Press, 1980), 164. The translation has been slightly modified. Italics in the original.

Notes   147

9. Jonas, *Imperative of Responsibility*, 18.

10. [Quoting a late poem by Hölderlin, "In lieblicher Bläue" ("... poetically, man/Dwells on this earth"); see Heidegger's commentary, "'... Poetically Man Dwells ...'" (1951), in Poetry, *Language, Thought*, trans. Albert Hofstadter (New York: Harper & Row, 1971), 213–27.—Trans.]

11. Illich, *Énérgie et Équité*, 68.

12. Gorz, *Ecology and Politics*, 77.

13. Lepage and Guery, *La politique de précaution*, 177–78.

14. Hans Jonas, *Le Principe Responsabilité: Une éthique pour la civilisation technologique* (Paris: Flammarion, 1995), 419 and 417. The emphasis is mine.

CHAPTER 4. THE AUTONOMY OF TECHNOLOGY

1. The mathematical framework is borrowed from information theory and the theory of automata networks. See M. Koppel, H. Atlan, and J.-P. Dupuy, "Von Foerster's Conjecture—Trivial Machines and Alienation in Systems," *International Journal of General Systems* 13 (1987): 257–64; also my article "Individual Alienation and Systems Intelligence," in Jean-Louis Roos, ed., *Economics and Artificial Intelligence* (Oxford: Pergamon Press, 1987), 37–40.

2. Jonas, *Imperative of Responsibility*, 32.

3. See Martin Heidegger, "The Question Concerning Technology" (1954), in *The Question Concerning Technology and Other Essays*, ed. and trans. William Lovitt (New York: Harper & Row, 1977), 287–317.

4. Dominique Bourg, *L'homme artifice: Le sens de la technique* (Paris: Gallimard, 1996), 85, 90. Bourg is referring here to two works by Ellul in particular: *La technique; ou, L'enjeu du siècle* (Paris: Armand Colin, 1954) and *Le système technicien* (Paris: Calmann-Lévy, 1977). [Both these works are available in English versions, under the titles *The Technological Society* (1964) and *The Technological System* (1980), respectively.—Trans.]

5. Jacques Ellul, *The Technological Society*, trans. John Wilkinson (New York: Knopf, 1964), 138; quoted by Bourg, *L'homme artifice*, 86. [Note that Ellul uses the French term *la technique* to refer not only to technology (its usual English translation) or to machines or procedures for achieving a particular purpose but to "the *totality of methods rationally arrived at and having absolute efficiency* (for a given stage of development) in *every* field of human activity" (xxv); it is therefore translated by Wilkinson literally as "technique," and in modifying contexts as "technical."—Trans.]

6. See Friedrich von Hayek, *Individualism and Economic Order* (Chicago: University of Chicago Press, 1948).

7. In my book *Le sacrifice et l'envie*, see the chapter on Smith (75–106) and the section of the chapter on Hayek that compares his views on imitation with those of Keynes (266–76).

148   Notes

8. See, for example, the model presented in André Orléan, "Money and Mimetic Speculation," in Paul Dumouchel, ed., *Violence and Truth: On the Work of René Girard*, trans. Mark R. Anspach (Stanford, CA: Stanford University Press, 1988), 101–12. Under certain conditions, the imitative dynamic is shown to converge on the unanimity of the group. These conditions entail the existence of a real interdependence among all the agents.

9. Jonas, *Imperative of Responsibility*, 32.

10. See Dupuy, *On the Origins of Cognitive Science*, 142.

11. See in particular the very widely noticed and discussed warning from one of the most brilliant living computer scientists, Bill Joy, that appeared in the April 2000 issue of *Wired*, "Why the Future Doesn't Need Us: Our Most Powerful 21st-Century Technologies—Robotics, Genetic Engineering, and Nanotech—Are Threatening to Make Humans an Endangered Species."

CHAPTER 5. DOOMSAYING ON TRIAL

1. See the article by Olivier Godard, "L'ambivalence de la précaution et la transformation des rapports entre science et décision," in Olivier Godard, ed., *Le principe de précaution dans la conduite des affaires humaines* (Paris: Éditions de la Maison des Sciences de l'Homme/INRA, 1997), 37–83; also the entry "Principe de Précaution" by Catherine Larrère in Canto-Sperber, ed., *Dictionnaire de l'éthique et de philosophie morale* (3rd ed., 2001), 1534–1537.

2. Lepage and Guery, *La politique de précaution*, 140.

3. Ibid., 136.

4. On November 1, 2001, Defense Secretary Donald Rumsfeld, addressing the "speed of progress" of the American military response to the September 11 attacks, emphasized that "the smoke at this very moment is still rising out of the World Trade Center" and the ruins are "still smoldering." On CNN, tape of Rumsfeld's comments was accompanied by images of the wreckage at Ground Zero, the epicenter of the tragedy. The anchorman, noting that sometimes it felt as if the attacks on the World Trade Center and the Pentagon had taken place a long time ago, urged viewers not to forget how recent they really were.

5. Proof that the metaphysics developed by Jonas is fully in agreement with mine on this cardinal point (and therefore innocent of the charge of panicky or naïve alarmism) may be found in the passage I quoted earlier, where he speaks of the need to grant "priority to well-grounded possibilities of disaster," as distinct from "mere fearful fantasies" (*Imperative of Responsibility*, 32).

6. Throughout this book I use the words "actual" and "actuality" in the philosophical sense of something that is realized rather than merely potential.

7. Statement made in April 1993 to the Conseil d'État by the French government's commissioner on the question of contaminated blood; see Olivier Godard, "Principe

Notes • 149

de Précaution et Responsabilité: Une Révision des Relations Entre Science, Décision et Société," in M. Neuberg et al., *Qu'est-ce qu'être responsable?* (Paris: Editions Sciences Humaines, 1997), 95. This formula subsequently served as the basis for many recommendations in other matters, notably with regard to mad-cow disease.

8. Jonas, *Imperative of Responsibility*, 37.

9. It will be recalled that the Dutch mathematician L. E. J. Brouwer's "constructivist" conception of truth (or rather of provability) led him to develop an intuitionist logic that denies the principle of the excluded middle and holds that the negation of a negation is not equivalent to an affirmation. [See Brouwer's controversial 1923 paper, "On the Significance of the Principle of Excluded Middle in Mathematics, Especially in Function Theory," translated (with addenda and corrigenda) in Jean van Heijenoort, ed., *From Frege to Gödel: A Sourcebook in Mathematical Logic, 1879–1931*, 3rd ed. (Cambridge, MA: Harvard University Press, 1976), 334–45.—Trans.]

10. The jurist Menno T. Kamminga persuasively argues that the precautionary principle was applied in international law with regard to violations of human rights well before environmental law perceived its usefulness; see his article "The Precautionary Approach in International Human Rights Law: How It Can Benefit the Environment," in David Freestone and Ellen Hey, eds., *The Precautionary Principle and International Law: The Challenge of Implementation* (The Hague: Kluwer, 1996), 171–86.

11. See Peter T. Saunders, "Use and Abuse of the Precautionary Principle," Institute of Science in Society (ISIS) Submission to U.S. Advisory Committee on International Economic Policy (ACIEP), Biotech Working Group, July 13, 2000; available online at http://www.i-sis.org.uk/prec.php.

12. Hans Jonas, *Das Prinzip Verantwortung: Versuch einer Ethik für die technologische Zivilization* (Frankfurt am Main: Insel, 1979).

13. Jonas, *Imperative of Responsibility*, 32.

14. Ibid., 31.

15. Ibid., 34. Translation slightly modified.

16. See Larrère, "Précaution," in *Dictionnaire d'éthique et de philosophie morale*.

17. Jonas, *Imperative of Responsibility*, 27–28.

18. Ibid., 23.

19. For a profound and mordant analysis of the follies to which such an attitude leads, see Monique Canto-Sperber, *Moral Disquiet and Human Life*, trans. Silvia Pavel (Princeton, NJ: Princeton University Press, 2008).

20. Jonas suggests, for example, that human beings, fortified by eschatological expectation, ought to be able "to accept as the necessary price of their physical safety a suspension of liberty in matters external to humanity"; see *Pour une éthique du futur*, 115.

21. Ibid., 24.

150　　　　　　　　　　　　　　　　　　　　　　　　　　　　Notes

22. "Philosophically, metaphysics in our time has fallen into disgrace," Jonas lamented, "but we cannot do without it; and so we must take our chances with it once more"; ibid., 90. Here Jonas was speaking exclusively from the vantage point of Continental philosophy.

23. Jonas, *Imperative of Responsibility*, 45. Italics in the original.

24. The French spelling of the biblical prophet Jonah's name is "Jonas."—Trans.

CHAPTER 6. PRECAUTION, BETWEEN RISK AND UNCERTAINTY

1. See David Fleming, "The Economics of Taking Care: An Evaluation of the Precautionary Principle," in Freestone and Hey, eds., *The Precautionary Principle and International Law*, 147–67. The same idea was taken up by Philippe Kourilsky and Geneviève Viney in their report to the French prime minister; see *Le principe de précaution*, 21.

2. Kourilsky and Viney, *Le principe de précaution*, 21.

3. The text of Law 95–101 may be found at http://www.legifrance.gouv.fr/affichTexte.do?cidTexte=LEGITEXT000005617673&dateTexte=20101124.

4. See John Maynard Keynes, *A Treatise on Probability* (London: Macmillan, 1921).

5. See Frank H. Knight, *Risk, Uncertainty, and Profit* (Boston: Houghton Mifflin, 1921).

6. Kourilsky and Viney, *Le principe de précaution*, 18.

7. Ibid.

8. Although his seminal work *Foundations of Statistics* appeared only in 1954, it extended the theory of expected utility formulated by von Neumann and Morgenstern in *Theory of Games and Economic Behavior* (Princeton, NJ: Princeton University Press, 1944) to include subjective probabilities.

9. A lottery is defined as a set of gains and losses to which a probability distribution is assigned. If lottery A is the set {one chance in two, I win 10; one chance in two, I win nothing} and lottery B is the set {I am certain to win 5}, then a linear combination C could be the set {one chance in four, I win 10; one chance in two, I win 5; one chance in four, I win nothing}.

10. See John Maynard Keynes, *The General Theory of Employment, Interest, and Money*, 4.13 (London: Macmillan, 1936), 170–74.

11. See Christian Gollier et al., "Scientific progress and irreversibility: An economic interpretation of the 'Precautionary Principle,'" *Journal of Public Economics* 75 (2000): 229–53.

12. Unquestionably the most famous of these is the Allais paradox. See Maurice Allais, "Le comportement de l'homme rationnel devant le risque: Critique des postulats et axiomes de l'école américaine," *Econometrica* 21 (1953): 503–46.

13. See Daniel Ellsberg, "Risk, ambiguity, and the Savage axioms," *Quarterly Journal of Economics* 75 (1961): 643–69. [The author of this paper worked at the time as a

Notes

consultant to the Defense Department, an experience he recounts in *The Doomsday Machine: Confessions of a Nuclear Planner* (New York: Bloomsbury, 2017).—Trans.]

14. See Itzhak Gilboa and David Schmeidler, "Maxmin expected utility with non-unique prior," *Journal of Mathematical Economics* 18 (1989): 141–53.

CHAPTER 7. THE VEIL OF IGNORANCE AND MORAL LUCK

1. In the hope of clearing up a misunderstanding that one finds everywhere (and especially, as we have seen, in criticisms of Jonas), let me repeat: *this in no way means that the player believes that "the worst" will in fact come to pass.* In the first place, there is not a single worst case, but one for each contemplated course of action. In the second place, it is not a matter of saying what the player *believes* about the *actual* future, but how he *reasons* in comparing *conditional* futures: 'If I did such-and-such a thing, this is what would happen.'

2. My Stanford colleague Marie Elisabeth Paté-Cornell, a foremost authority on the evaluation and management of risk, has persuasively argued that aversion to uncertainty is a source of economic and social wastefulness; see "Uncertainties in Risk Analysis: Six Levels of Treatment," *Reliability Engineering and System Safety* 54 (1996): 95–111. This aversion may lead policymakers to allocate too many resources to the prevention of poorly understood risks, for which no reliable probabilities are available, and not enough resources to the prevention of well-understood risks. (In France one thinks of the relatively small amount of resources devoted to preventing traffic accidents or to reducing the consumption of tobacco and alcohol.) From Paté-Cornell's argument I conclude that one cannot construct an ethics adequate to a time of catastrophes on the basis of a psychological disposition such as uncertainty aversion.

3. See John Rawls, *A Theory of Justice*, §24 (Cambridge, MA: Harvard University Press, 1971), 136–44.

4. See Bernard Williams, "Moral Luck," in *Moral Luck: Philosophical Papers, 1973–1980* (Cambridge: Cambridge University Press, 1981), 20–39.

5. François Ewald, "Précaution, incertitude et responsabilité," part of the entry on technological risks in *Encyclopaedia Universalis* (Paris: Encyclopedia Universalis, 2001), online, no pagination. The emphasis is mine.

6. Jonas, *Pour une éthique du futur*, 103.

7. I observe with amusement that the debate among international experts on reducing greenhouse-gas emissions that led to the Kyoto Protocol gave rise to a "no-regrets strategy," the inspiration for which is exactly the opposite of what I have just urged, for it enjoins nations to doing nothing that they would regret having done if it should turn out, once the veil of ignorance imposed by the unpredictability of the future has been lifted, that the doomsayers were wrong. See Stephen R. Dovers and John W. Handmer, "Ignorance, Sustainability, and the Precautionary Principle: Towards an Analytical Framework," in Ronnie Harding and Elizabeth C. Fisher, eds., *Perspectives on the*

Precautionary Principle (Sydney: The Federation Press, 1999), 167–89; also Jean-Charles Hourcade, "Précaution et approche séquentielle de la décision face aux risques climatiques de l'effet de serre," in Godard, ed., *Le principe de précaution dans la conduite des affaires humaines*, 281–93.

CHAPTER 8. KNOWING IS NOT BELIEVING

1. Jonas, *Imperative of Responsibility*, 7–8. Apart from the italicized first word of this extract, the emphasis is mine.

2. Ibid., 29. Again, the emphasis is mine.

3. See the very impressive argument developed by David Fleming, "The Economics of Taking Care," in Freestone and Hey, eds., *The Precautionary Principle and International Law*; David Pearce, "The Precautionary Principle and Economic Analysis," in O'Riordan and Cameron, eds., *Interpreting the Precautionary Principle*, 132–51.

4. This point is strongly emphasized by O'Riordan and Cameron, "The History and Contemporary Significance of the Precautionary Principle," in their edited volume *Interpreting the Precautionary Principle*, 13–15.

5. Jonas, *Imperative of Responsibility*, 29.

6. Harding and Fisher very efficiently dispose of this illusion, sometimes cherished by scientists themselves, in their introduction ("Uncertainty, Risk, and Precaution: Exploring the Links") to the fourth part of *Perspectives on the Precautionary Principle*, 163–65. Gérard Mégie, the world's foremost expert on the stratospheric ozone layer, has demonstrated that scientific research can sometimes increase uncertainty, rather than reduce it; see "Incertitude scientifique et décision politique: Le cas 'historique' de l'ozone stratosphérique," in Godard, ed., *Le principe de précaution dans la conduite des affaires humaines*, 215–43. In the works I have already cited by André Orléan on mimetic speculation, more realistic assumptions about the economy refute the belief that a better understanding of market mechanisms will make their workings more predictable.

   In the case of the chemistry of the upper atmosphere, as in that of the economy, the reason for what may at first appear to be a paradox is that scientific progress depends on improvements in modeling. Where the reality being modeled is complex, the model's faithfulness to reality implies that it must itself be complex. I use the word "complex" here in its technical sense: a model is complex if its behavior cannot be fully specified in advance (owing to the impossibility of integrating the differential equations it contains and to its sensitivity to initial conditions), so that the simplest way to predict the behavior of a model is to observe the physical system that it is supposed to represent! John von Neumann was the first to perceive this paradoxical inversion of the hierarchical relationship between a natural object and its model. See my discussion of this theme in *On the Origins of Cognitive Science*, 137–43; obviously it is bound up with the problem of technological autonomy, which we examined in chapter 4.

Notes

7. Telling examples of this state of affairs may be found in the debates over the destruction of the stratospheric ozone layer and mad-cow disease. On the first, see the subtle analysis by Gérard Mégie in the article cited in the previous note; on the second, the no less fascinating essay by Marie-Angèle Hermitte and Dominique Dormont, "Propositions pour le principe de précaution à la lumière de l'affaire de la vache folle," in Kourilsky and Viney, eds., *Le principe de précaution*, 341–86.

8. See Dieter Birnbacher, *Verantwortung für zukünftige Generationem* (Stuttgart: Reclam, 1988). [Translated from the French version, *La responsabilité envers les générations futures* (Paris: Presses Universitaires de France, 1994), 143, corrected by the author.—Trans.]

9. See especially Dovers and Handmer, "Ignorance, Sustainability, and the Precautionary Principle," in Harding and Fisher, eds., *Perspectives on the Precautionary Principle*; Daniel Bodansky, "The Precautionary Principle in U.S. Environmental Law," in O'Riordan and Cameron, eds., *Interpreting the Precautionary Principle*, 203–28.

10. Particularly in French, German, and English. Overwhelmed by the torrent of articles and books on the subject in French, and convinced that American scholars had taken little interest in the question, I imagined at the outset that I would find nothing valuable in English. The seminar that I taught at Stanford in the spring of 2001 rapidly persuaded me that I was wrong. Thanks in particular to the work of Australian and British authors, what has been written on the precautionary principle in English is impressive for both its rigor and its depth. The references I give here testify to this fact.

11. Lepage and Guery, *La politique de précaution*, 51.

12. Kourilsky and Viney, *Le principe de précaution*, 18.

13. Hermitte and Dormont, "Propositions pour le principe de précaution à la lumière de l'affaire de la vache folle," in Kourilsky and Viney, eds., *Le principe de précaution*, 349.

14. This point is well documented in Bodansky, "The Precautionary Principle in U.S. Environmental Law," in O'Riordan and Cameron, eds., *Interpreting the Precautionary Principle*.

15. At this juncture it may be useful to recall a point of logic. From the proposition "John knows that the worst is going to happen," it may be inferred that the worst will in fact happen; but the same inference cannot be made from the proposition "John believes that the worst is going to happen." One cannot know something that is false, but one may falsely *believe* something to be true.

16. Lepage and Guery, *La politique de précaution*, 16.

17. Ibid., 70. The emphasis is mine.

18. See Fleming, "The Economics of Taking Care," in Freestone and Hey, eds., *The Precautionary Principle and International Law*; also O'Riordan and Cameron, "The History and Contemporary Significance of the Precautionary Principle," in O'Riordan and Cameron, eds., *Interpreting the Precautionary Principle*.

19. According to a French intelligence expert, Admiral Pierre Lacoste, although American officials had a great deal of information available to them after the 1993 attack on the World Trade Center in New York, they were paralyzed by the scale of what needed to be done. In the same vein, it is chilling to superimpose a map of population density on a map showing all the industrial installations in France alone that are at risk. But it is hard to see what can be done. Catastrophe is therefore not regarded as a real possibility. The same is true with regard to the refusal to take seriously the possibility of a major economic catastrophe, on a national or global scale. [The original French edition of this book, it will be recalled, appeared more than six years before the global economic crisis of 2008.—Trans.]

20. The French film critic Samuel Blumenfield, writing in *Le Monde* on October 9, 2001, ("Hollywood digère l'attaque du 11 septembre") noted: "This terrorist attack draws upon our [collective] memory, fed in part by Hollywood's cinema of destruction, which now suddenly finds itself honored as the prophet of a tragedy that it *had portrayed many times, without ever believing it possible*" (my emphasis).

CHAPTER 9. MEMORY OF THE FUTURE

1. Larrère, "Précaution," in Canto-Sperber, ed., *Dictionnaire d'éthique et de philosophie morale*, 1536.

2. Jonas, *Imperative of Responsibility*, 6.

3. The reduction of moral philosophy to a state of lethargy in French universities and intellectual life more generally has not been without consequence. Today the French are in the position of having to relearn how to think in normative terms—in the first place, by following the example of moral philosophers writing in English, who have not ceased to develop and refine their thinking while at the same time bringing a critical attitude to bear upon it.

4. Samuel Scheffler, "Individual Responsibility in a Global Age," *Social Philosophy and Policy* 12 (Winter 1995): 219–36.

5. Jonas, *Imperative of Responsibility*, 6.

6. Jonas, *Pour une éthique du futur*, 83–84. Emphasis in the original.

7. Ibid., 82. Again, the emphasis is the author's.

8. Jean-Paul Sartre, *Existentialism Is a Humanism*, trans. Carol Macomber (New Haven, CT: Yale University Press, 2007), 29–30, 26, 25. The emphasis, except in the final instance, is mine. [Macomber's mistranslation of the final sentence of the first of these passages has been silently corrected.—Trans.]

9. See Henri Grivois, *Naître à la folie* (Paris: Les Empêcheurs de Penser en Rond, 1992).

10. Jonas, *Le Principe Responsabilité*, 16. The emphasis is mine.

11. Ibid., 12. Emphasis in the original, except for the final two italicized phrases.

Notes 155

12. Dieter Birnbacher takes up the same idea when he writes: "The horizon of responsibility toward the future vanishes only at the point where the causal lines that stretch from the present to the future, if one considers them in the perspective of the present, dissolve or merge so indissociably with one another that it is no longer rational to assume a causal relation between the activity of the present time and future states of the world. . . . But to be able to determine how far the causal effects of current action actually extend, one must first place oneself in the perspective of the future—and this perspective cannot be adopted definitively" (*La responsabilité envers les générations futures*, 142–43).

CHAPTER 10. PREDICTING THE FUTURE IN ORDER
TO CHANGE IT (JONAH VS. JONAS)

1. David Fleming, in a quite remarkable essay that I have already referred to more than once, "The Economics of Taking Care," in Freestone and Hey, eds., *The Precautionary Principle and International Law* (see especially 161–64), deplores the loss of a "sense of the future." In spite of the rise of forecasting, he observes, the future is seen as something that is at once unknowable and at the mercy of determinisms about which we can do nothing. Such a society, he adds, "does not need the past." Fleming concludes: "the sense of time itself—the sense that the future has a reality, and that it has claims on us—is in danger of extinction." As Bill Joy would say, however, "the future doesn't need us."

2. Some philosophers—and not the least eminent (e.g., Aristotle)—do not accept the principle of the reality of the future.

3. An important case is that of propositions that bear upon the future action of an agent assumed to enjoy free will ("future contingents" in scholastic terminology).

4. The author of the Book of Jonah probably lived in the fifth century B.C., or even later, which is to say during the post-exilic period. The attribution of Jonah's adventures to Jonah, son of Amittai, who lived during the time of Jeroboam II, King of Israel (783–743), and who is mentioned in 2 Kings 14:25, appears to be without historical foundation.

5. See, for example, James D. Newsome, Jr., *The Hebrew Prophets* (Atlanta: John Knox Press, 1984), 196–200.

6. This point is persuasively argued by John F. A. Sawyer, *Prophecy and the Prophets of the Old Testament*, rev. ed. (New York: Oxford University Press, 1993), 125–27. See also Hans Walter Wolff, "Prophecy from the Eighth through the Fifth Century," in James Luther Mays and Paul J. Achtemeier, eds., *Reinterpreting the Prophets* (Philadelphia: Fortress Press, 1987), 14–26, which shows that condemnation of sinners never comes without a forecast of things to come and that, if only one of these two elements is present in prophetic discourse, it is invariably the announcement of what the future holds in store. Gene M. Tucker, in an essay in the same collection, "Prophetic Speech," 27–40, observes that punishment is generally not described by the prophet as a threat

156   Notes

that will be carried out if people continue to engage in licentious behavior, but as a reality situated in the future, typically the near future. Seldom does a conditional element intervene: it is not "People of Israel, here is what will happen *if* you continue to live in sin"; it is rather "You are living in sin. Here *therefore* is what is going to happen," or else "Here is what is going to happen *because* you are living in sin." The Book of Amos is typical in this regard.

7. See Deuteronomy 18:9–14.

8. See ibid., 18:15–20. The word used in the Bible for "prophet" is *nabi'*. Significantly, the first Greek translations translated the Hebrew term not by *mántis* (diviner or seer), but by *prophátas*, which is to say interpreter.

9. Jonas, *Imperative of Responsibility*, 120.

10. David K. Lewis, "Counterfactual Dependence and Time's Arrow" (1979), reprinted with postscripts in *Philosophical Papers*, vol. 2 (Oxford: Oxford University Press, 1986), 38. The emphasis in the penultimate sentence is mine.

11. Jorge Luis Borges, "The Creation and P. H. Gosse," in *Selected Non-Fictions*, ed. and trans. Eliot Weinberger (New York: Penguin, 1999), 223. Here Borges is commenting on the chapter of John Stuart Mill's *System of Logic* (1843) dealing with the law of causality.

CHAPTER 11. PROJECTED TIME AND OCCURRING TIME

1. Herbert A. Simon, "Bandwagon and Underdog Effects and the Possibility of Election Predictions," *Public Opinion Quarterly* 18 (1954): 245–53. This article gave rise to a faintly ridiculous debate over an incidental point with Norwegian mathematician Karl Egil Aubert in the pages of *Social Science Information*.

2. Jean-Jacques Rousseau, *The Social Contract*, 2.3, in Roger D. Masters and Christopher Kelly, eds., *The Collected Writings of Rousseau*, 12 vols. (Hanover, NH: University Press of New England, 1990–2007), 4:147.

3. Cf. Isaiah 55:10–11: "'For as the rain comes down [saith the Lord], and the snow from heaven, and do not return there, but water the earth, and make it bring forth and bud, that it may give seed to the sower and bread to the eater, so shall My word be that goes forth from My mouth; it shall not return to Me void, but it shall accomplish what I please, and it shall prosper in the thing for which I sent it.'"

4. Jonas, *Imperative of Responsibility*, 113–14. Emphasis in the original.

5. It was unfortunately within the framework of this traditional metaphysics that Hans Jonas went looking for a solution to his dilemma. But if he failed to grasp that something altogether different was required, he succeeded in defining clearly the terms of the problem. "For here," Jonas remarked, "where men theorize about men, and publicly at that, *the existence of the theory, being itself a historical factor, changes the conditions of the object of knowledge*. Because it acquires causal power itself in order to

Notes

157

help its truth to gain reality, [and] thus with intent contributes to the coming true of its prognoses, it could belong to the *self-fulfilling prophecies*: its being right in the end would not prove its truth, but rather its power over the minds by which it becomes the cause of particular actions" (*Imperative of Responsibility*, 115; the emphasis in the second instance is mine).

6. In the case of the tragic hero, it might be argued that what existentialists call bad faith and analytical philosophers of mind call self-deception is at work: the protagonist holds a certain belief (namely, that he is free to act and to make events occur) while simultaneously holding the opposite belief (that he is subject to fate). For a subtle examination of this idea that draws upon two classic examples, see Robert Doran, "*Alazon*: Tragic Self-Deception in Œdipus Rex and *Macbeth*," Stanford University memo, 1999.

7. Jorge Luis Borges, "The Mirror of the Enigmas," in *Other Inquisitions, 1937–1952*, trans. Ruth L. C. Sims (New York: Simon and Schuster, 1968), 128.

8. From the title of Borges's story "The Garden of Forking Paths" (1941), in *Collected Fictions*, trans. Andrew Hurley (New York: Penguin, 1998), 119–28; the phrase is quoted by Lewis in "Counterfactual Dependence and Time's Arrow," *Philosophical Papers*, 2:36.

9. Ibid., 127. [Hurley's version has been modified.—Trans.]

10. See Jean-Pierre Dupuy, "Counterfactual Consequences," paper delivered at the Conference on Rationality and Intentions, University of Amsterdam, October 15–16, 1999.

11. In the jargon of economists, agents are therefore said to be "price-takers."

12. The economics of convention is devoted to applying this concept to a variety of fields, from money to labor relations [see *Revue économique* 40, no. 2 (1989), special issue on "L'économie des conventions"]. It is inspired by David K. Lewis's book *Convention: A Philosophical Study* (Cambridge, MA: Harvard University Press, 1969).

13. One might say, by analogy with the notion of price-takers, that agents in this respect are "past-takers."

14. See the major work published in 1984 by Jules Vuillemin, available in a revised English edition as *Necessity or Contingency: The Master Argument* (Stanford, CA: Center for the Study of Language and Information, 1996). The other axioms as reconstructed by Vuillemin are: 1) the past is irrevocable; 2) the impossible does not logically follow from the possible; and 3) that which is can't not be as long as it is.

15. Carl von Clausewitz, *On War*, eds. and trans. Michael Howard and Peter Paret (Princeton, NJ: Princeton University Press, 1976), 181.

16. Christine M. Korsgaard, "Morality as Freedom," in *Creating the Kingdom of Ends* (Cambridge: Cambridge University Press, 1996), 164.

17. For a more detailed treatment of concepts that I am able to present here only in summary form, see Jean-Pierre Dupuy, "Common Knowledge, Common Sense," *Theory*

158 Notes

and Decision 27 (1989): 37–62; "Two Temporalities, Two Rationalities: A New Look at Newcomb's Paradox," in Paul Bourgine and Bernard Walliser, eds., *Economics and Cognitive Science* (New York: Pergamon, 1992), 191–220; and "Philosophical Foundations of a New Concept of Equilibrium in the Social Sciences: Projected Equilibrium," *Philosophical Studies* 100 (2000): 323–45. Many of the same ideas are also discussed in Jean-Pierre Dupuy, ed., *Self-Deception and Paradoxes of Rationality* (Stanford, CA: Center for the Study of Language and Information, 1998).

18. Jean-Paul Sartre, *Being and Nothingness: An Essay on Phenomenological Ontology*, trans. Hazel E. Barnes (New York: Philosophical Library, 1956), 522 (translation modified).

19. Compare these two propositions: "If I bought an apartment on ritzy Avenue Foch in Paris, I would *have had to be* rich"; and "If I bought an apartment on ritzy Avenue Foch in Paris, I would be poor" (because buying it would ruin me). By reasoning back to what would "have had to be," projected time violates the first axiom of the Master Argument. The past is not irrevocable, it is not fixed; present action has a counterfactual power over the past. This power is obviously not causal; no physical law is violated.

20. Roger Guesnerie, *L'économie de marché* (Paris: Flammarion, 1996), 75. This formula reflects the spirit of rational expectations theory.

CHAPTER 12. THE RATIONALITY OF DOOMSAYING

1. Compare Lessing's use of the mythical account in *Laocoön: An Essay on the Limits of Painting and Poetry* (1766).

2. Jonas, *Imperative of Responsibility*, 28. The emphasis is mine.

3. Jonas, *Pour une éthique du futur*, 101. Emphasis in the original.

4. Jonas, *Imperative of Responsibility*, 38–39. The emphasis at the end is mine.

5. Friedrich Nietzsche, *On the Genealogy of Morals*, Second Essay ("'Guilt,' 'Bad Conscience,' and the Like"), trans. Walter Kaufmann and R. J. Hollingdale (New York: Vintage Books, 1967), 57, 58. Emphasis in the original.

6. See David K. Lewis, "Devil's Bargains and the Real World," in Douglas MacLean, ed., *The Security Gamble: Deterrence Dilemmas in the Nuclear Age* (Totowa, NJ: Rowman and Allanheld, 1984), 141–54. Among the other philosophers participating in the debate, one must cite Gregory Kavka, David Gauthier, and Jean Hampton.

7. I have taken up this matter in detail in my book *Penser la dissuasion nucléaire* (Paris: Presses Universitaires de France, 2002), as well as in a report prepared several years earlier for the French Ministry of Defense, "La dissuasion nucléaire: Essai d'évaluation au regard de l'éthique et de la prudence" (February 1998).

8. Dominique David, then Secretary General of the Fondation pour les Études de Défense Nationale in Paris, quoted by *The Christian Science Monitor* (June 4, 1986).

9. I use this term in the sense it has in the theory of just war: all non-combatants are said to be innocent. In French nuclear doctrine, modestly described as "deterrence of the

Notes

strong by the weak," the strike is purposely designed to annihilate an enemy's urban centers and civilian population. This is (or was?) its distinctive feature.

10. See Gregory Kavka, *Moral Paradoxes of Nuclear Deterrence* (New York: Cambridge University Press, 1987), 19–21.

11. As David K. Lewis emphatically put it, "*You don't tangle with tigers*—it's that simple"; see "Finite Counterforce," in Henry Shue, ed., *Nuclear Deterrence and Moral Restraint: Critical Choices for American Strategy* (New York: Cambridge University Press, 1989), 51–114.

12. Steven P. Lee, *Morality, Prudence, and Nuclear Weapons* (Cambridge: Cambridge University Press, 1996), 248.

13. Bernard Brodie, *War and Politics* (New York: Macmillan, 1973), 430–31. The emphasis is mine.

14. As noted earlier, the billions spent throughout the world to avoid the Y2K bug gave rise to a similar suspicion. Such instances could easily be multiplied.

15. See Schelling's book *The Strategy of Conflict* (Cambridge, MA: Harvard University Press, 1960), which gave a second wind to game theory.

16. This idea attained a pinnacle of sorts with Richard Nixon's behavior as president during the Vietnam war. "I call it the Madman Theory, Bob," Nixon told his White House Chief of Staff, H. R. Haldeman. "I want the North Vietnamese to believe I've reached the point where I might do *anything* to stop the war. We'll just slip the word to them that 'for God's sake, you know Nixon is obsessed about Communism. We can't restrain him when he's angry—and he has his hand on the nuclear button'—and Ho Chi Minh himself will be in Paris in two days begging for peace." Quoted in H. R. Haldeman (with Joseph DiMona), *The Ends of Power* (New York: Times Books, 1978), 83.

17. Note that one must still inform one's adversary of the machine's existence! In Kubrick's film, the Soviets neglected to warn the Americans that they had invented and deployed a Doomsday Machine.

18. Readers interested in more detailed discussions may consult two of my articles cited earlier, "Philosophical Foundations of a New Concept of Equilibrium" and "Two Temporalities, Two Rationalities" (see the notes to chapter 11).

19. The discontinuity encountered at $\varepsilon = 0$ suggests that something like an uncertainty principle, or rather an indeterminacy principle, is at work here. The probabilities ε and $1-\varepsilon$ behave like probabilities in quantum mechanics. Moreover, the fixed point must be conceived in projected time as the *superposition* of two states, one the accidental *and* preordained occurrence of the catastrophe, the other its non-occurrence. It is not possible here to pursue this line of thought any further. I am indebted to my former Stanford colleague Aviv Bergman for his suggestions.

20. We need also to say more clearly what distinguishes a strategic accident from a fatality or foreordained accident. The first involves the probability of a conditional proposition of the type: "If you were to attack me, I would reply in such a way that the escalation of

violence would destroy both of us." Here we find ourselves in occurring time, in which uncertainty attaches to an intentional act. A foreordained accident, on the other hand, involves the probability of a conditional of the type: "If the catastrophe were inscribed in the future, I would make it causally possible by acting in such and such a fashion." Here we are in projected time, which accounts for the backtracking form of this curious conditional. The apocalyptic destiny "already" belongs to the actual world, as a fatality, precisely. It is our responsibility to make it improbable, by trying to refrain from acting in such a fashion as to make it causally possible.

21. See Ameisen's extraordinary book *La sculpture du vivant: Le suicide cellulaire ou la mort créatrice* (Paris: Seuil, 1999).

22. Ibid., 13.

Index

A

actualization of the future, 132

Allais, Maurice, the Allais paradox, 150n12

Ameisen, Jean-Claude, programmed cell death, 142

Amos, 118; Book of Amos, 156n2

Arendt, Hannah, 22

Aristotle, 126, 128, 155n2; on phronesis, 63; on practical syllogism, 73

Atlan, Henri, 37

Aubert, Karl Egil, 156n1

August 4, 1914, x

autonomous production, 8–9, 27, 29, 85

B

balance of terror, 133, 136

Barnier law, 65, 70, 87

Bayesian, 64, 68

Beck, Ulrich, risk societies, 21

Berger, Peter, *Pyramids of Sacrifice* (1974), 22

Bergson, Henri, xii, 51–52, 56, 93, 105, 106–8, 126, 128; "The Possible and the Real" (1930), xi; *The True Source of Morality and Religion* (1918), x–xii

Birnbacher, Dieter, 89, 155n12

Blumenfield, Samuel (1963), cinema of destruction, 154n20

Borges, Jorge Luis, 95, 114, 156; "Garden of Forking Paths," 121, 142

Bourg, Dominique, 38–39

Brodie, Bernard, 137–40

Brouwer, L. E. J. (1881–1966), 149n9

Burke, Edmund, xi

C

Caiaphas, 21

calculus of probabilities, 4

capitalism, 13–14, 23

catastrophes, x–xiii, 6, 27, 48–52, 56–57, 65, 82, 85, 90–92, 97, 100–112, 118–19, 122, 131–32, 136–27, 141, 151n2, 154n19, 159–60nn19–20; catastrophic events, 55, 86, 98, 129, 138, 140; catastrophists, x, 55, 79, 82, 88–89

causalism, 120–21; causal dependence, 121–29; causal effects, 52, 84, 100, 119, 120, 155n12, 156–57n5, 158n19; causality, 156–57n5; causally, 102, 120, 122, 159–60n20; circular causality, 37

161

Civil Code (France), 80, 81
climate, 4; change, 25, 27, 35, 50, 99; warming, 6
Cold War, 24, 48, 133–34
conditional futures, 102, 112, 151; conditional hypothesis, 50; conditional propositions, 52, 113, 116, 123, 159–60n20; conditionals, 128, 129, 135, 140, 155–56n6, 159–60n20
consequentialism, 19, 20, 76, 98–101; doctrines of, 19; ethics of, 21; rationality in, 135; utilitarian variant of, 145n12
coordination convention, 124
counterfactual future, 102, 113, 120–22; counterfactual conditionals, 128–29; counterfactually independent and dependent, 120–24; dependence, 113, 120–21; prices as counterfactually independent, 123
counterproductivity, 8, 9, 13, 15, 16, 27–28, 30–34, 37, 47
Cronus, Diodorus, Master Argument, 126, 158n19
Cuernavaca, 9

D

decision-making, 4, 65, 88; decision tree, 120
decision theory, , 68, 71, 72, 73, 75, 106
deconstruction, 13, 58
Derrida, Jacques, 58
Descartes, René, 53
destructive evolution, 93, 108
determinism, 118; chaos in, 87; system of, 87
deterrence, 133, 134–41, 158–59n9
de Tocqueville, Alexis, 10, 11, 19
detour, 9, 18, 19, 132; logic of the, 14–18
Deuteronomy: 18:21–22, 111
developed world, 11
Domenach, Jean-Marie, 7
doom, 35, 44, 52, 55, 58, 59, 95, 111, 112, 131, 142; doomsayer and doomsaying, ix, x, 8, 11, 48, 50, 53, 56, 110, 114, 129, 131, 134, 138, 140, 142, 151n7

Doran, Robert, 157
Dubos, René: 28
Dumont, Louis, 15, 145n6

E

economics, 4, 8,19, 20, 21, 23, 69, 71, 116, 119, , 151n2, 154n19, 157n12; of convention, 157n12; environmental, 5; macroeconomics, 47; mathematical, 41
ecosystems, complexity of, 85–87
Ellsberg, Daniel, 71–72, 79
Ellul, Jacques, 38–39, 147n5
Elster, Jon, 14, 145n7
enlightened doomsaying, x, 48, 142
equality, 11
equilibrium, 28, 39, 41, 123
ethics, 3, 5, 14, 19, 20, 21, 57, 58, 70, 71, 75, 84, 97, 98, 101, 102, 135, 144n2, 151n2; deontological, 19, 20, 21, 76
Ewald, François, 80–81

F

fatalism, 26, 107, 115, 118, 127
Fermat, Pierre de, 4
first-step fallacy, 14
Fleming, David, inverse principle of risk evaluation, 92, 155n1
France, ix, x, 6, 9, 10, 18, 28, 38, 51, 63, 80, 116, 129, 134, 151n2
Frankfurt School, 13
future indicative, 107

G

games of chance, 4, 66
Gauguin, Paul, 80–82
Germany, declaration of war on France, ix, 51
Gilboa, Itzhak, uncertainty aversion, 71–73
Gorz, André, *Ecology as Politics* (1980), 30, 34
Great War, xi
Ground Zero, 148n4
Guery, François, 7, 89–90
Guesnerie, Roger, state economic planning in France, 129, 140

Index

H

Hegel, Georg Wilhelm Friedrich, 24

Heidegger, Martin, 10; *Entschlossenheit*, 128; Heideggerian critique of rationality, 13, 38

Hermitte, Marie-Angèle, 90

heteronomous production, 8–9, 27, 29, 85

Hobbes, Thomas, 56–57

Huygens, Christiaan, 4

I

Illich, Ivan, 8–10, 13, 15, 19, 37, 47, 57, 85, 132, 145n9; *Medical Nemesis* (1974), 26–30, 32

imitation, 39–44; mimic, 44, 71, 127, 139

industrialization, 13, 27

industrial society, 4, 8, 10, 13, 18–19, 24, 32–34, 47, 132

instrumental rationality, 13–16, 19, 22

Isaiah 55:10–11, 156n3

J

James, William, xi, 143n1

Jesus, 21, 110

Jonah, 59, 109; Book of, 95, 109–19, 150n24, 155n4

Jonas, Hans, 11, 26, 30, 34–35, 38, 43, 53, 73, 82, 84–86, 89, 97–99, 100–103, 107, 109, 112–14, 118–19, 125, 127, 144n2, 148n5, 149n20, 150n22, 156n5; *The Imperative of Responsibility* (1979): 55–59, 97–98; futurology or not-yet-existent, 132; heuristics of fear, 55–56, 89, 92, 101, 133, 141; on Marxism, 118; as prophet of doom, 131–32

Joy, Bill,155n1

K

Kamminga, Menno T., 149n10

Kant, Immanuel, xi, 19, 20, 22, 58, 70, 76, 79, 100–101, 102, 112, 128

Kavka, Gregory, 135

Keynes, John Maynard, 40, 66, 69,

Knight, Frank, 66, 71

Koppel, Moshe, 37

Korsgaard, Christine, 128

Kourilsky, Philippe, the Kourilsky-Viney report, 64, 66–67, 90, 144n2

Kubrick, Stanley, 139; Doomsday Machine, 159n17; *Dr. Strangelove* (1964), 139

Kyoto Protocol, 151n7

L

Lacoste, Pierre, French intelligence expert, 154n19

Laplace, Pierre-Simon, 87

Larrère, Catherine, 56, 97

Lee, Steven, existential deterrence, 137

Leibniz, Gottfried Wilhelm, 21, 24, 50, 106, 112, 128; *Monadology* (1714), 14; *Theodicy* (1710), 14

Lepage, Corinne, 34, 49–50, 91–92

Lewis, David K., 112–13, 120–21, 133, 159n11

lottery, 4, 72, 83, 139, 150n9

M

MAD (mutually assured destruction), 48, 133–36, 139, 141

Marx, Karl, 23, 44; alienation, 31; Marxism, 13, 31, 118, 122–23

Massé, Pierre, ozone layer, 129

maximization, 14, 19, 20, 21, 68

Mégie, Gérard, 152n6

metaphysics, 51, 52, 57, 58, 82, 93, 105–08, 112, 114, 126, 128, 148n5, 150n22, 156n5; metaphysics of occurring time, 139, 141; of projected time, 129, 132, 138, 140; of time and free will, 113, 118–20

midrashim, 110

mimetic rivalry, 141

minimax method, 50, 64, 75, 76

modernity, 10, 11, 24, 31

moral luck, 79, 80, 82

morality, x, 20, 57, 80, 99, 133, ; common sense morality, 19, 21, 98–100, 135; Kantian morality, 76, 100

N

Nietzsche, Friedrich, 128, 132

Nixon, Richard, 159n16

Nozick, Robert, 20, 21
nuclear apocalypse, 24, 135–36
nuclear destruction, 106
nuclear deterrence, 133–38, 159n16
nuclear energy, 50
nuclear peace, 24
nuclear power plants, x, 49, 67, 84
nuclear war, 3, 133, 136

O

occurring time, 121–27, 132, 138–39, 141, 159–60n20
Oedipus, 141
Orléan, André, 148n8, 152n6

P

Pascal, Blaise, 4, 50, 53, 66; the "half-clever," 35
Paté-Cornell, Marie Elisabeth, aversion to uncertainty, 151n2
path dependence, 43
Plato, *Theaetetus* and *Meno*, 91
political ecology, 13
polling, 117
Ponge, Francis, 100
Popper, Karl, 53
precaution, 6, 30, 49, 55, 59, 63–69, 71–73, 83, 86–90, 105, 144n2,
precautionary policy, 84
precautionary principle, 48, 49, 55, 63–65, 68–70, 87–89, 91, 100, 133, 144n2, 149n10
prediction, 38, 50, 52, 100, 107–10, 116–17, 120, 125, 127, 131
prevention, xii, 64–65, 67–69, 73, 86, 89, 91, 105–6, 111, 114, 127, 132, 136–38, 151n2
price-takers, 157n11, 157n13
probability theory, 66, 87
projected time, 121, 126–29, 132, 138–42, 158n19, 159n19, 159–60n20
prophátas, 156n8
prophets, 109–11, 119; biblical prophets, 110, 117–18, 131, 155n6; of doom, 8, 44, 52, 55–56, 110–12, 131; of happiness, 44; revolutionary prophecy, 118; self-fulfilling prophecy, 119

R

rational choice, 4, 63–65, 69, 106; collective rationality, 6; procedural rationality, 6; rationalist extremist, 8; substantive rationality, 6; theory on equilibrium, 123
Rawls, John: *A Theory of Justice* (1971); 98; veil of ignorance, 76–79, 82, 151n7
risks, 3–7, 66, 69, 75; economists, 83; prevention, 64; societies, 21; zero, 49
Rousseau, Jean-Jacques, 19, 117
Rumsfeld, Donald, 148n4
Russell, Bertrand, 106

S

sacrifice, 23, 146n16; *Sacrifice* (Hubert and Mauss, 1899), 22
Sartre, Jean-Paul, xii, 100–101, 128
Savage, Leonard, 4, 63, 69, 71; subjective probabilities, 68
scapegoats, 59, 71
Scheffler, Samuel, common sense morality, 98–100
Schelling, Thomas, rational to mimic irrationality, 139
Schmeidler, David, and Itzhak Gilboa, uncertainty aversion, 71–73
science: objectivity, 6; revisionist view, 7
September 11, x, xi, 11, 92, 121, 133, 148n4
Shakespeare, *Troilus and Cressida*, 113
Simon, Herbert, 116; polling "fixed point," 116–17
simulation, 108
Smith, Adam, the invisible hand, 15, 23
Soviet Union, 106
specularity, 123–24
Spielberg, Steven, *Saving Private Ryan*, 146n16
Spinoza, Baruch, 128
Star Wars, 133

T

technological project, 10
technological systems, 85
tragic hero, 157n6
Tucker, Gene M., 155–56n6

Index 165

U

Ullmo, Jean, 8
uncertainty, 4, 6–7, 50, 64–73, 75–80,
83–84, 86–90, 103, 136, 139, 144n2,
151n2, 152n6, 159n19, 159–60n20
United States, 106, 137
utilitarianism, 20–21, 78

V

Viney, Geneviève, the Kourilsky-Viney
report, 64, 66–67, 90, 144n2
von Clausewitz, Carl, 127
von Foerster, Heinz, 9, 37–39, 44, 86;
theorem of, 119, 123
von Hayek, Friedrich, 23, 39–40, 43; self-
exteriorization, 39, 43–44
von Neumann, John, 4, 44, 63, 106, 152n6
Vuillemin, Jules, 157n14

W

Weber, Max, disenchantment of the world,
13
Williams, Bernard, 80, 82
Wolff, Hans Walter, 155n6
World Trade Center, 51, 107, 148, 154n196
World War II, 106

Y

Yom Kippur, 110
Y2K bug, 143n5, 159n14